"Ours is an age sadly confused about much and greatly confused about marriage. Robert and Gloria Stella have written a clear, lucid and practical work on the basic building block of society and they have done it while avoiding the traps of pompous religiosity and smug condescension. I recommend this book to everyone who hopes to make a real marriage work in the midst of a confused and wayward culture."

-DR. MARK RUTLAND

Founder, Global Servants and The National Institute of Christian Leadership

Former President, Oral Roberts University and Southeastern University

Author, New York Times Best Seller *Relaunch*

"The traditional notion of marriage is slowly headed toward extinction. Our culture is plagued with ideals of how relationships should work in the 21st century, but our family unit is in disarray more so now than ever before. Robert and Gloria take couples back to the basics in *CounterCulture Marriage*, reestablishing God's authority on marriage and making happy marriages a possible option."

-MARK COLE

CEO, John Maxwell Enterprise

"In *CounterCulture Marriage*, Robert and Gloria challenge the cultural norms that plague today's marriages. With personal stories and scripture, they present the argument for marriage done God's way. If you are looking for something more in your marriage, I encourage you to read this book. I believe your marriage will be blessed as a result of reading it."

-MARCUS MECUM

Senior Pastor, 7 Hills Church

D1273148

"Where was a book like *CounterCulture Marriage* 31 years ago when Donna and I first married straight out of high school? Five kids later and the rat-race that the world offers as the gospel, our marriage has survived only by the grace of God. Unfortunately, countless other couples have suffered loss and devastation because of the culture that is the example before them. Through this book, Robert and Gloria teach solid, biblical principles to build a lasting marriage and how to counter what the culture offers. Brilliantly written, *CounterCulture Marriage* is a picture of relational transparency, through real-life examples."

-CHIP WOODALL

Founding and Lead Pastor, Christwalk International Ministries, Inc

"*CounterCulture Marriage* is for today's couples. Easy to understand concepts that are in touch with issues marriages face today. Robert and Gloria Stella understand culture, but more importantly, God's plan for marriage!"

-ANDY BRENT MS, LPC

Director of Counseling, Free Chapel

"If you have been looking for a fresh, cutting edge marriage book, LOOK NO MORE! After serving in marriage ministry for many years, I have reviewed countless books for marriages. Authors, Pastor Robert and Gloria Stella, have been given a gift to understand the challenges of married couples today in this fast-paced world of information and social media. This book is informative, fun and effective to bring lasting change in a home when the principles are applied."

-REBECCA KEENER

TV Host, "Always More" and Co-Host, "The Christian View"

Author, *The Marvelous Madness of Motherhood*

FOREWORD BY JENTEZEN FRANKLIN

ROBERT & GLORIA STELLA

FINDING #HAPPILYEVERAFTER IN A #MARRIAGESUCKS WORLD

COUNTER|CULTURE

MARRIAGE

IDFL PUBLISHING

#legalstuff

CounterCulture Marriage
Finding #happilyeverafter in a #marriagesucks world

Published by Edifi Publishing
3446 Winder Highway
Suite M195
Flowery Branch, GA 30542

info@counterculturemin.com
www.counterculturemin.com

Edited by Hannah Price and Ruth Woodson
Cover design & layout by Gloria Stella
Cover photo by Amanda Hamlin Photography

ISBN: 978-0-692-09127-2

Printed and bound in the United States of America

10 9 8 7 6 5 4 3 2 1

This book is dedicated to all the couples who have experienced the pain and dissatisfaction of living life by the rules of our current culture - and dare to believe that there's more to life and marriage than simply surviving.

CONTENT

ACKNOWLEDGEMENTS

To our children - Urijah, Samuel and Liayah: Each of you was birthed representing a different aspect of God's promises and ushered us into three different seasons of our lives. We pray that just as you have influenced the masses even as babes, that our shoulders will serve as your launching point. We love you all incredibly.

To Robert's parents - Paul and Merrie Brundage: Thank you for your unmatched support in all of our pursuits. We miss you Dad and we are blessed to have you in our lives Mom. We love you.

To Gloria's parents - John and Sarah Meyer: Thank you for showing us what commitment in a marriage looks like and for allowing us to work through our struggles instead of bailing us out even when you wanted to. You've made us stronger and we love you guys for it.

To our Pastors - Jentezen and Cherise Franklin: Thank you for encouraging us to dream dreams and pursue God passionately. Thank you for believing in us and taking ownership of what God has called us to do. You have preached us through every high and low we've experienced. We love you both.

To our Executive Pastor - Tracy Page: Thank you for your leadership and guidance throughout this process and for taking the time to provide invaluable feedback for the words written in these pages.

To our mentors - Chip and Donna Woodall: Thank you for ushering two teenagers into the call of God on their lives. We love the whole Woodall clan!

To our biggest advocate - Becky Keener: Thank you for empowering us to influence marriages. It was you who gave us the title "CounterCulture Marriage" in 2008 and continually pushed us to develop the idea through every phase until it finally became this book. This book would not exist without you.

To our first marriage teachers - Bert and Malissia Sasser, Dr. and Mrs. Tsai and the late Ben and Fran Thigpen: When we were the first teenagers to get married from the college group, you guys stepped up and committed to teaching the young marrieds Sunday school class - even when many times, we were the only ones that showed up. Your faithfulness produced fruit.

To our first supporter - James Glutting: Thank you for your incredible friendship and thank you for being the first person to financially contribute to this ministry.

To our editors - Ruth Woodson and Hannah Price: Thank you for the endless hours you spent editing these words - making them less churchy and more relevant, restructuring paragraphs and eliminating so many unnecessary words. This book is more enjoyable to read because of you guys.

To the Young Marrieds group circa 2008 to 2013: You guys know who you are - the core group that served as our guinea pigs at the inception of the CounterCulture study and offered so much great feedback and support as we've continued on this journey.

To our Lord & Savior - God, Jesus and the Holy Spirit: No words could ever come close. Thank you for your Word to serve as our foundation. Thank you for orchestrating our lives allowing us to simply enjoy the ride. Mostly, thank you for your unconditional love that carries us through every season, covers our every failure and is responsible for our every success. We pray that our lives serve as a living sacrifice for you and we never cease to give you all the Glory.

FOREWORD

One of the greatest challenges of the 21st century are marriages that can stand the test of time. I will even go so far as to say that healthy, lasting marriages are the glue that holds families together and bring stability, not just to a home, but to a nation. The carnage left in the wake of broken homes serves as a reminder that we must cherish, protect, and nurture our marriages in a day and age where anything goes. We have to stand our ground and hold that holy hill of matrimony if we are to see God's purpose come to life with the life mate God gave you.

CounterCulture Marriage is everything the title says. We live in a culture that not only encourages separation and experimentation, but values personal gain over commitment and sacrifice. So many marriages end in divorce and the culture would tell you that is the new normal. But it has never been God's normal. There is a better way.

In every marriage situation there is hope. I have counseled many couples where it appeared reconciliation was impossible only to see God take two willing and open hearts and do a miracle. But I have also seen marriages end over the most petty circumstances. The difference was that the marriages that stayed together had a plan; a roadmap out of the dark places and into the light. *CounterCulture Marriage* is that roadmap, whether you are just getting started and want to navigate away from the rocks or if your ship is sinking with no help in sight.

I want to encourage you to walk through each carefully crafted chapter and to be open to all God has to say. If you will allow the Holy Spirit to guide you through the pages ahead, He will speak to you and shine light on the dark places and show you a better way.

I know of no greater blessing than a happy marriage where there is strength for the battles, encouragement for the challenges, and comfort for the storms of life. Marriage was created because two are stronger than one, and because there is great joy in uniting your life with another and finding common purpose. And I know of no greater teacher than God's Word. *CounterCulture Marriage* will show you the truths in God's Word that have stood the test of time in every culture, in every century, and in every tongue.

-JENTEZEN FRANKLIN
Senior Pastor, Free Chapel
Author of New York Times Best Seller *Fasting*

INTRODUCTION

INTRODUCTION

Marriage is a good thing. Yet, the vast majority of today's movies, TV shows, tabloids and social media content present something very different.

Early in our marriage, we used to spend many evenings curled up on the couch enjoying the latest family sitcoms. We'd laugh at the characters, the ridiculous situations they encountered and shake our heads at the seemingly exaggerated dynamics of their TV marriages. But it didn't take us long to realize that the marriages portrayed in those shows, weren't as ridiculous as we thought. In fact, shortly after getting involved in the marriage ministry, it became clear that most marriages, even in the church, reflected many of the same negative stereotypes that we saw on TV.

By default, we tend to absorb what we see and hear in the media and subconsciously apply it as a guideline in our own lives. As a result, many couples live in the false stereotype that marriage is nothing more than a trap of boring and sexless days keeping us from living the life we really want. But marriage, the way God intended, is a beautiful notion that frees us to be secure in who we are, inspires us to dream bigger and fulfills us in every area of our lives (yes, even sexually). Thankfully, God doesn't leave us guessing. He gives us clear guidelines in scripture to show us how to do marriage God's way.

When we began teaching these concepts to other young couples however, we were met with some resistance. Let's face it, the way God wants us to handle things is usually the complete opposite of what makes sense to us. But we truly believe that if you'll make the effort to live by these guidelines God has provided for even a short period of time, you'll be surprised at how much of a difference it can make. We have found that even non-Christian couples that follow these Biblically-based guidelines (whether they know they are doing it or not) find themselves in a happier and healthier marriage as well.

"Happily ever after" isn't just something an author says to end a fairytale. It's something that can actually exist in "real life". On the other hand, "happily ever after" doesn't necessarily mean flawless perfection. In our own marriage, as you'll see transparently unfold in this book, we've been through incredible hardships from "living in the real world". We've had to work through healing from seasons of self-inflicted heartbreak and personal failures. Even today, we still have our fair share of ups and downs.

We are, after all, flawed humans and this is real life in a real world full of other flawed humans and unfair (and sometimes self-inflicted) hardships. If you're looking for a book that will hand you "happily ever after" on a silver platter, wrapped in a bow with the promise of never crying another tear - this isn't the book for you. However, if you're looking for a way to make "happily ever after" the essence of what embodies the culture of your marriage – even amidst the trials and tribulations of real life, then read further.

Matthew 7:24-27 tells the story of the "wise man who built his house on the rock: and the rain descended, the floods came, and the winds blew and beat on that house; and it did not fall, for it was founded on the rock." It wasn't a matter of if the floods would come, it was a matter of whether or not the house would still be standing when the waters receded. If you wait until your marriage is in trouble before you decide to build it on the rock, one unexpected blow could bring your marriage to an end. But if you take the time to build a strong marriage now, even when the winds start attacking, your comeback can be stronger than your setback.

In this book, we've translated, in culturally-relevant language, what it means to build your marriage "on the rock" in hopes that it will lead you to your end destination – a marriage founded on God - where marital bliss, adventure, joy, peace and purpose remain constant despite circumstances – a happily, ever, after.

THE BUSINESS OF MARRIAGE

#friendship

culture • Marriage is an endless to-do list that keeps you from happiness
counter-culture • Marriage is an endless friendship that fosters happiness

one

THE BUSINESS OF MARRIAGE

For many of us, when we were first diving into a serious dating relationship with our spouse, we did so because we enjoyed their company. We enjoyed their company so much so that we were excited about the prospect of making them our husband or wife. That's a pretty heavy commitment and it says something about how we felt about that relationship on a social level. Many of us would've claimed that our spouse was our best friend.

Then five, fifteen or more years later you look at your spouse and think to yourself that you don't really know them or enjoy their company anymore. They are more like roommates...a roommate you have committed your entire life to sharing your space with. From the day you started planning your wedding or the day that the first baby came into the house, your lives suddenly revolve around a massively growing to-do list revolving around your kids, finances, careers and the hundreds of other things that tend to fill up your days. Life and your marriage become somewhat of a business and somewhere along the way, you may have lost touch with the friendship you had with your spouse when your relationship began. And who can blame you? You barely have time to take a shower, forget having time to actually socialize with people. Isn't this why we love texting so much? It's quick, to the point and we can skip the "hi, how are you doing?" nonsense...after all, every second counts.

Although this fast-paced mentality is great for our productivity output (most of the time), it certainly doesn't do much for our marriages. Nearly every aspect of our marriage is built on our ability to stay connected to our spouse.

SIGN ON THE DOTTED LINE

Marriage isn't a contract you signed on your wedding day and it's not a commitment that you are obligated to fulfill out of fear of being excommunicated from the Christian church. Your marriage is a covenant – a commitment you fulfill through your relationship with someone. Whereas contracts and commitments can be with someone with whom you have very little or no relationship with a covenant is fueled by relationship. We need to make an extra effort to ensure that our relationship with our spouse is fueled by our love for them and not just out of our legal or religious obligation to them.

No one wants to lose that special connection they once had with their spouse and yet, in our culture, that connection has been reduced to a single stage in our marriage that is expected to fade until we are left with nothing left but a binding contract.

THE HONEYMOON STAGE

For the purposes of this book, let's define the "Honeymoon Stage" as the time when we first got married and we enjoyed being together and were genuinely interested in our spouse's dreams and interests. This would be the time when our relationship with our spouse was more about enjoying each other rather than just handling the logistics of a life together.

When you and your spouse first started dating and fell in love, most likely there was an air of excitement and a genuine interest in who they were. You couldn't get enough. What's his favorite color? What is her favorite movie? What music does she listen to? What are his biggest dreams? What drives her forward? What holds him back? What is his family like? You wanted to know anything and everything about that person.

You didn't just want to know about them, you wanted to be with them every second of every day. You weren't so concerned with the circumstances and setting having to be just perfect – it didn't matter – what mattered was that you were in their presence.

I (Robert) remember when Gloria and I were dating (and very broke) that we would find any excuse to be around each other. We were content sitting in a car at the Sonic Drive-In restaurant parking lot talking about nothing. We would even talk on the phone for hours…again, usually about nothing.

Perhaps you and your spouse were the same way at one point - and now, it seems that if you can't find the money to get out of the house for a dinner and movie there just isn't any point in "connecting." After all, you both live in the same house and see each other all the time. But let's remember that there is a huge difference between being around each other and actually connecting.

Connecting with your spouse is something that seems to get lost in the routine of life. This is why our culture has decided that the "honeymoon stage" is only a temporary phase. However, what if we told you that the honeymoon phase only ends when you let it?

Much like when you come to know Jesus as your personal Lord and Savior, when you first take that huge step and make that life-changing decision, your whole life changes and you have a zeal and passion to get to know and grow closer to God. But if you take a look around the Christian community, you'll notice that most of the people who have stayed faithful to their Christian faith, who initially were "on fire" for God, seem to have fallen into a routine and religious lifestyle rather than a passionate growing relationship with their Lord and Savior. I think we can all agree that it is not God's intention for his followers to ever fall into a religious routine when it pertains to their relationship with Him. And yet, it happens. Primarily because we let it.

The same thing happens in our marriages. We have a very difficult time believing that God called two people together and gave them a zeal and passion for each other only for that connection to flicker out after a few years. God intends for us to stay connected and genuinely intrigued and interested in our spouse throughout our entire marriage.

The honeymoon stage shouldn't exist. That certainly doesn't mean that life will be sunshine and roses every day. This is real life and in real life there are overwhelming to-do lists, problems, disagreements and tragedy. But it does mean that it is possible to stay connected with your spouse through those difficult seasons. It's possible to still feel excited about your spouse twenty, thirty or more years later and it's possible to still feel connected and in love even when your marriage is no longer new.

RE: CONNECT
Reconnecting with your spouse is a process that involves logistical effort. When priorities or deadlines are placed on us from external sources, we tend to take them seriously because there are typically immediate consequences. However, when it comes to our marriages, it's easy to procrastinate because the consequences of a marriage that is neglected present themselves gradually. In order to be fulfilled in our marriage – and our life, we have to decide to make our marriage a priority and make the logistical arrangements necessary for that to happen.

Re: Learn
Research shows us that we change dramatically during our lifetime. Our likes, dislikes, dreams, interests and our personalities[1] are constantly changing. The vast majority of the cells in our bodies completely replace themselves from every few days to every several years[2] so that who we were biologically several years ago is almost completely different from who we are today.

Something as simple as a hatred towards spaghetti could easily turn into a treasured favorite seven years later. A person who used to be passive and easy-going can become aggressive and the life of the party several years down the road. So, although we may feel like we learned all about our spouse several years ago, we need to be in a constant state of relearning about them to stay connected.

From the age of 16, I (Robert) dreamed of climbing the corporate ladder in the auto dealership industry. I got my first job at a Toyota dealership detailing cars when I was 18 and then spent the next several years working my way through a slew of dealership positions until I eventually landed in the world of corporate auto finance at Capital One. Then things started to shift. Fast-forward a couple more years and I found myself going into full-time ministry and leaving my honest days as a used car salesman behind (#sarcasm). It wasn't just my occupation that changed, but who I was changed. With that, my dreams changed and so did my interests.

Now imagine if Gloria and I stopped connecting and lost the desire to get to know each other after the first few months. When Gloria and I got married, it was a dream we both shared that one day we'd own a chain of auto dealerships. If ten years later I walked through the doors and told her I was leaving the car industry and going into full-time ministry, I think she would be wondering what happened to the guy she married and would feel like she didn't know me anymore.

Unfortunately, that is where many married couples end up. But if you make an effort to stay connected and "chit-chat" regularly about your opinions, dreams and interests, there will always be something interesting and new to learn about your spouse and you won't find yourself taken off-guard when there is a major shift in who your spouse becomes.

In fact, you can learn the value of this pretty quickly with a simple exercise. Simply ask your spouse a few open-ended questions: What's something interesting that happened today? What would you do with a million dollars? What's your dream vacation? What's something you wish you knew how to do? You never know where those conversations will carry you, but they will help you rebuild the friendship within your marriage.

Just as asking a few questions can open up a world of conversational possibilities, finding time to reconnect and relearn your spouse doesn't have to be some major event scheduled on the calendar. If we make it such a big deal then it puts the pressure on our spouses to come up with something "new and interesting" to tell about themselves and it becomes another task on the to-do list that we have to fulfill for our marriages to be successful. Instead, we're suggesting a lifestyle adjustment.

Make it a point to talk about random things regularly - things that have nothing to do with the finances, kids, jobs, etc. Talk about how much you love or don't love the current weather season or talk about a car that drives down the road that you really like or show your spouse the video of the latest technology reveal that caught your eye.

Why do we reserve these personal interests for ourselves? If something interests you, tell your spouse. On the other hand, if something interests your spouse, let them tell you with excitement and engage in the excitement with them.

Re: Engage

The mind is a powerful thing and if you really want to, you can choose to develop an interest in what your spouse is interested in. Put aside the mentality that it's "just not me" or "that's really dumb". Over time, we become like the people we most associate with[3], eventually developing the same habits and interests. We can facilitate that same growth with our spouse. Be willing to explore things that your spouse loves with the intention of growing those similar interests.

I (Gloria) didn't grow up in a sports house. My dad is a complete computer nerd (and takes pride in that fact). The closest I got to seeing a sports game was when I had to attend football games in high school because I was part of the flag corps in our marching band...and even then, I was only present, I didn't actually watch the game. Robert, on the other hand, is a huge sports fan...Miami Hurricanes football being his favorite sports pastime.

For several years I made no attempt to engage in his football activities and football became something I grew to disdain and be jealous of because I felt like he was spending so much time and energy dedicated to football instead of being dedicated to me. A popular saying states, "if you can't beat 'em, join 'em" and I finally decided to stop fighting his interest in football and make a genuine effort in joining in on his excitement for it.

I love learning, being quizzed and trivia. So one night out, Robert spent a couple hours telling me all about the top players and coaches and the history of Miami Hurricanes football. Then he spent some time quizzing me on said facts. He thought it was a cheesy idea, but I enjoyed it. Then we spent a few weeks taking sporadic shopping trips to the mall for the cutest Miami Hurricanes shirt and hat I could find. At that time, Robert wasn't a huge fan of shopping (although that has changed dramatically since then), but he enjoyed those shopping trips and I enjoyed spending time with him. Then several years later, the kids and I had a lot of fun making replica turnover chains to wear during the games. And when it came time to fill out March Madness brackets, I decided to make one too. Of course, my bracket was based on which mascots I liked the most and that particular year the Blue Devils won - so needless to say, my bracket was a little off.

I will say that my passion for the actual game didn't increase much, but I learned to understand the game and I found my own genuine ways to connect with Robert through his fascination with sports and it did facilitate more of a friendship atmosphere within our marriage. Football became less of a point of dissension and more of a way for us to have fun together. And the more fun Robert had with me, the more he took an interest in what I loved doing and the more we connected as friends.

These topics may seem trivial to you, especially if and when you and your spouse have bigger fish to fry, but if one of those fish is the feeling that you've lost (or are losing) that connection with your spouse that you once had, you may be amazed at how effective connecting on such unimportant matters can help bring you and your spouse together on a deeper level. Casual and friendly conversations usually deepen into more intimate and serious ones.

Re: Date

Dating is a fundamental aspect of staying connected and staying friends. After all, you're not likely to be friends with someone that you don't like to spend time with and contrary to popular belief, dating doesn't have to equal spending money.

One of my (Gloria) favorite date memories is during one of those seasons when we were flat broke. We set up a folding table next to our Charlie Brown Christmas tree and I set up the Scrabble board while Robert cooked us two bowls of ramen noodles. We put on some nice music and spent the evening talking and laughing. It was a very stressful time in our lives but being able to find the time to have a "date" was rejuvenating.

Even without a babysitter or money, there are ways to create a date if you're willing to think out of the box. It's more a matter of making it a priority in your life.

Re: Imagine

Never stop dreaming and never stop dreaming together. God has called us to greater things and a greater purpose than just getting married and repopulating the earth. He has given each of us a purpose and a dream as individuals and as couples. What we can accomplish on our own is minimal compared to what we can accomplish when we are united with our spouse in the purpose that God has placed on our lives.

My (Robert) purpose lies within full-time ministry, while Gloria is called to the entertainment industry. Although our dreams may seem to be in two entirely different facets of the world, it will take the both of us dreaming together in order for God to accomplish what He has called us to accomplish.

God will never call you to a purpose that causes you to separate from your spouse. You should never view your purpose or dream as just "your" dream or just "your spouse's" dream. God's timing is perfect and most often, He works through seasons in ways beyond what we can comprehend. It's not a competition of who gets to work towards their individual purpose more. There are seasons when Gloria spends most or all of her work time committed to our dream in ministry. Then there are seasons when we spend much of our mental, emotional and physical energy committed to a film project.

Like Gloria and I, you and your spouse may have dreams and be called to purposes in two completely separate industries. Dreaming together doesn't necessarily mean that you have to have the same dream, but that your unique individual callings merge into one purpose. I don't just support and encourage Gloria in her purpose, but I adopt her dream as part of my own dream. Her vision becomes part of my vision. Her purpose becomes part of my purpose and vice versa.

As couples, we need to learn to work together towards the purpose that God has placed in our lives for that season and never settle for a routine existence.

FRENEMIES

We can simultaneously be making efforts to reconnect with our spouse and at the same time be sabotaging those efforts. If we want to make real progress, we not only have to do the right things, but we have to stop doing the wrong things.

Uptight Much?

There are times when you can just tell that someone is wound-up so tight they're just trying not to explode. I (Gloria) call them "high-strung mommies" but they can be high-strung daddies, husbands, business owners, etc. They don't have to say a word, but the vibe they give off is one of frazzled overload.

This is especially true with couples who walk into church and were obviously fighting. There is no affection and no real smiles. They might walk into church a couple feet apart but they might as well have walked into different buildings. Sometimes the husband will try to grab the wife's hand to try to loosen up the situation or hide the fact that they were fighting, but she quickly snatches it away.

One such Sunday morning, I (Gloria) remember walking into the church so angry I couldn't even fake a smile. That morning, everyone I passed probably thought I was mad at them. I was so determined to hang on to my anger that it was impossible for me to worship, but tears started streaming down my face. I know that anyone who saw me must have been thinking, "oh wow, look at Gloria, she's so in love with Jesus she can't hold it in." But the truth was that I was so mad at Robert I couldn't hold it in and all that anger had nowhere else to go except out my tears…. especially since I couldn't yell at him in the middle of a worship song or storm out of the church building.

I don't even remember what that fight was about, but truthfully, it probably wasn't a big deal. Might have been in that moment, but if I would have let myself loosen up, it was probably something I could have easily let slide off my back and enjoyed my family that morning.

Particularly for women (or at least for me), it's so easy to get into a mode of uptightness once we get started down that road. We can end up approaching everyone and every situation with a disgruntled attitude and snap at anyone who crosses our path – no matter if they actually deserved it or not. Not everything your spouse does wrong is a big deal. They are not perfect and neither are you.

You can choose to reprimand your spouse every time the trash isn't taken out the second you asked or you can choose to thank them for remembering to do it before the trash man came. If they didn't take the trash out on-time, it's still not a big deal…the trash will come again next week. It's not the end of the world. It may take some effort, but we can choose to be less uptight about the little things so that we are more enjoyable to be around. Your spouse doesn't want to choose to be around you if all you do is yell at them for something. And that can go either way – for husbands and wives.

We understand that not everything is a laughing matter, but so many things are and if we would learn to laugh during the situation, it would be far easier to connect with our spouse.

For instance, your 3-year-old son spilling the milk all over the kitchen floor because he wanted to fix himself a drink is not life-threatening. Yes, it's probably a little frustrating and it might cost you a good 5-10 minutes of clean-up, but you could choose to get angry about it or remember that he won't be that cute forever and it'll be a story to tell twenty years from now when you're writing your first book.

The same goes for your spouse. The best time to let yourself laugh? How about during an intense argument about nothing? Some arguments really aren't a laughing matter, but most of the time, you can bicker and argue for so long that you don't even remember what you were arguing about in the first place.

Give yourself and your spouse permission to laugh if something funny happens during the argument. Don't laugh at your spouse. That wouldn't be nice. But there are many times in an argument that something is laughable. Maybe you're screaming faster than your brain can keep up and you seriously flub-up a word. Both you and your spouse stop yelling because you both know it was funny but you're both afraid to laugh because you want to hold onto your anger. Don't do that. Stop taking yourself so seriously and laugh a little.

> *"A cheerful heart is good medicine, but a broken*
> *spirit saps a person's strength."*
> *-Proverbs 17:22 (NLT)*

Instead of running out the door or letting the situation get the best of you, try letting yourself laugh through some situations and loosen up. The more critical and disgruntled that you approach life the weaker you'll become and the harder things will seem.

Grading & Comparing

When you first married your spouse, you were probably pretty happy with them. Hopefully you didn't take note of all the better options out there. Your spouse was your best option and you were going to get married and ride off into the sunset.

Many times, we can start to get critical when we start taking notice of what other spouses are doing or look like and how other marriages are operating. Especially in this social media age where people only post the good things, it's easy for you to start obsessing about how your spouse or your marriage could be better.

There is nothing wrong with wanting to improve yourself or your marriage. In fact, that's kind of what we were hoping for when we started writing this book. Maturing, improving and bettering yourself is a sign of growth, but when it becomes an obsession, it can zap the joy and friendship out of your marriage.

It's one thing to take an honest evaluation of where you and your marriage stand or to want to go to classes, read books and get counseling. It's an entirely different thing when it's all you and your spouse seem to do.

If you find that you are spending most of your time grading yourself and your marriage against what you see other couples do or what you read in the many marriage articles online, you may be missing the point. Self-help books are great, marriage books are beneficial, but if all you are doing is trying to make you, your spouse and your marriage perfect, then you'll be missing out on the "happy" part of a happy marriage. You can read all the marriage books you want, but you can easily spend so much time trying to perfect your marriage that you end up forgetting to enjoy it. If you can't learn to just enjoy hanging-out with your spouse without checking "reconnect" off your daily to-do list, it may be a long road to happy.

Unbalanced

Your marriage is not like everyone else's marriage. Your individual personalities are different, your chemistry is different, your culture is different. The advice and approach you find in many marriage resources can be helpful, but don't try to force a strategy or method to your marriage if it doesn't fit.

Of course, there are Biblical foundations for marriage that should be applied for a successful marriage, but the logistics of how you get there or the details of how it is applied may vary from marriage to marriage. Take the time to discuss perspectives that you learn with your spouse and discover what works for your marriage.

For instance, Gloria and I (Robert) have a very definite, scheduled date night once a week. It's rarely ever cancelled and we make sure to leave the house during that time. That is what works for us and keeps us connected. However, I would be hesitant to state as a fact that "every marriage has to have a date night once per week in order to be successful." Your spouse may work out of town the entire week and so having 2-3 date nights in one weekend is what's necessary to stay connected. On the other hand, you may be a couple without children and have the opportunity to connect over a peaceful, kid-friendly dinner at home every night and so an official "date night" may not be absolutely necessary every week. Find what works for your marriage.

> *"One hand full of rest is better than two fists full*
> *of labor and striving after wind."*
> *—Ecclesiastes 4:6 (NASB)*

Balance is key to everything in life. When it comes to marriage advice you run across, we suggest that you apply what is Biblical, use advice that is attainable, and archive what is inapplicable at the time. When it comes to the stressful period of your life, learn to laugh and take a break.

When it's One-Sided

So what do you do when you're the only one that seems to want to take steps toward improving the friendship aspect of your marriage? You do what you can. You start taking an interest in your spouse's interests. You start adopting their dreams. You start connecting with them. You start loosening up. Even if your actions are not reciprocated, you'll be planting seeds and your spouse will begin to take notice.

Only one of you needs to have hope for a better or happier marriage to get the ball rolling. It may not happen overnight, but overtime, if you'll do what you can do, God will handle what you can't do.

REMOVING STRESS

Stress has become somewhat of a buzzword in our culture. The amount of learning resources, medications and cures available are unreal. It's difficult to talk about building a friendship with your spouse when life seems so stressful that all we can manage to do is survive one day at a time. Being able to rekindle a friendship with our spouse is not just about bringing the "fun" back into the marriage. It also provides us with balance in our relationship with our spouse and our perspective on the stresses of life.

Get a Fresh Perspective

If you are stuck on a project or experiencing debilitating stress, it's a popularly accepted remedy to step away from that project and do something else so you can go back to that project with a fresh perspective[4]. We believe the same is true in our marriages.

Like most couples, Robert and I (Gloria) live a fast-paced life. During one specifically stressful season, we were both at a breaking point. Robert was working 60+ hours a week in a high-demand ministry and I was juggling five different projects ranging from film production and design projects to a full-time contracted business consultation project. Throw in two young children and a nursing newborn and our stress-levels were beyond capacity. Every interaction we had for several weeks was laced with intense hostility towards each other. And almost every hostile jab turned into a major fight. We were at each other's throats constantly, which only added to the stress of that season.

Finally, enough was enough. During a final meltdown, we both knew that all the other high-demand deadlines needed to be put on pause and we needed to make our marriage a priority. We had gotten to the point that we couldn't stand being around each other. Instead of leaning on each other for support during such a stressful season, we were using each other as verbal punching bags. We had created a culture in our marriage of having to "put up with each other" rather than joining together on this journey called life.

We started forcing quality time into our weekly schedules – whether that was spending all night chit-chatting after the kids went to bed or getting away for several hours with just the two of us. We really couldn't afford to lose any more sleep or take any time off at the height of our career deadlines, but it was either those externally-imposed demands or it was our marriage. We had to make a choice.

Thankfully, almost immediately we noticed the difference. When we started spending just a few hours a week focusing exclusively on just having "fun" with each other, we invited an atmosphere of friendship into our marriage. So even when we went back to all those same stressful situations during the week, we weren't stuck in a cycle of hostile attitudes toward each other. We stopped seeing each other as the enemy and started interacting with each other as if we were on the same side. Instead of fighting each other about every problem that arose, we found a way to join forces and work together to fight the problems.

Our life circumstances didn't change. The stress factors stayed intact. The kids still had their tantrums, deadlines didn't stop and we still had to find the money to pay the bills. But our perspectives changed. Stresses that used to be immovable mountains because that's all our life was consumed with became temporary problems that we knew would pass. We had found a way to remind ourselves that there was more to life than problems and stresses. There were things in life that we could enjoy, explore and laugh about. There were things about each other that we still liked and in light of the 80+ years we plan to live on this earth, the problems we were facing during that season seemed small in comparison.

That's the beauty of a perspective shift. When we are zoomed in to our little space and time of existence, that's all we can see and everything is given far more importance than it should really be given. But when you zoom-out and see the entire world and the timeline of humankind in comparison to the time and space we take up, we realize that the things we stress out about are negligible most of the time.

Trusting God

What if the key to handling stress was to not have it at all? We know that sounds pretty close to impossible, but God's intention is for us to do what we know to do and trust Him to fill in the gaps…thus eliminating the need to be stressed.

It's far too easy for us to be consumed with everything going on around us today and be concerned with all that we can imagine happening ten years from now. We have to remember that all God really requires of us is to stay focused on our relationship with Him and what tasks He's given us to complete today and He'll take care of the results.

> "Do not worry then saying, 'What will we eat?' or 'What will we drink?'
> or 'What will we wear for clothing?' For the Gentiles seek all these things;
> for your Heavenly Father knows that you need all these things. But seek
> first His kingdom and His righteousness, and all these things will be added
> to you. So do not worry about tomorrow; for tomorrow will care for itself.
> Each day has enough trouble of its own."
> —Matthew 6:31-34 (NASB)

What this verse does not say is that we can do whatever we want and because we claim that Jesus is our savior everything will turn out hunky-dorey. Quite the contrary. We must make our relationship with God a priority - surrendering every aspect of our lives to Him, living a lifestyle that is always seeking to please Him. If we do that, we don't need to worry so much about the solutions to our problems. When we get the revelation that obedience is up to us and the results are up to God, our stress and the pressure to perform immediately begins to decrease.

This doesn't necessarily mean that we just skip through a happy field of flowers and pretend like the grass isn't on fire and nipping at our heels. Gloria and I (Robert) have been through some very tough seasons in our life – some of which centered on major financial misfortunes. We understand that pretending a bill doesn't exist doesn't mean that the bill collectors don't come knocking. Pretending the doctor's diagnosis is a lie doesn't mean the illness goes away. However, this verse has proven to be true in our lives in every circumstance.

Your first thought in any stressful situation should be to take it back to God and pray for clarity and direction. Make sure that your perspective is in line with God's word regarding your situation.

Secondly, you still have to handle the logistics of life the best you know how. Discuss a plan of action with your spouse. Figure out a worst-case scenario solution given the resources available to you today. God gave us brains so we can think through things on our own and wisdom so we can think through things correctly. Thankfully, for us, we've never had to truly carry-out our worst-case scenario plan because somewhere, somehow, God gave us a brilliant idea in the middle of the night or left money on our windshield (literally) or our "worst-case scenario" ended up being a blessing rather than a curse. Believing that God will come through in the end does not mean that we don't have to move forward with what He has already made available to us. It doesn't mean that we don't have to still apply for jobs if we suddenly find ourselves unemployed or go through the treatment if we are diagnosed with an illness. We can't limit how God chooses to provide.

We heard a story many years ago about a town that came under the threat of a destructive flood. Local officials sent out an emergency warning giving all the residents time to evacuate their homes. There was one man in the town who chose to stay, sincerely believing that God would save him.

As the flood waters began seeping into his home, a neighbor with a pick-up truck stopped by and offered to drive the man to safety, but the man refused, stating that God would save him. The flood waters forced the man to sit on his roof where eventually a boat would come passing by and offered the man safe passage. Again, he refused stating that God would save him. Finally, the water level left the man floating without a foundation. A rescue helicopter flew by and sent down a ladder so the man could climb his way to safety, but again he refused, still believing God would save him. Finally, he died.

When he reached heaven, he asked God why He did not save him. After all, he believed with all his heart that God would be faithful. God responded that He had sent the man a warning to avoid the situation altogether. Then He sent a pick-up truck, a boat and a helicopter and the man refused all of them.

This story reminds us that God will provide, but we cannot confine God's provision to what we view as a "miracle" in our minds. If you and your spouse are financially struggling, it's great to believe that God is capable of putting a few thousand dollars in your mailbox, but don't think it's not also possible for God to provide an opportunity for you to downsize. If you are struggling with a teenager on the brink of rebellion, you can pray and believe that God shields them from the wrong choices and influences and keeps them from ever experiencing a rebellious path, but what may happen is that God protects them from permanent harm and brings them back to Him with a spirit of humility and a renewed passion for the purpose that God has for their lives.

The point is, life is full of unexpected circumstances and that especially holds true for a life lived for Christ. We have to remember that we cannot see the final picture or force something to be a success. What we can do is grow in our relationship with God, believe that He orders our every step, utilize the resources we have, focus on what needs to be handled today - and He will control the final outcome. If we can embed that deep into our hearts, it will release much of the stress that we feel in our lives and in our marriages.

FIND EACH OTHER IN THE VALLEY

If you consider the landscape of a valley, you'll notice that the sheer nature of the valley is that it comes down to one point. If you and your spouse are on top of each mountain, you are exposed to the many cares, opportunities and problems of the present and distant world and it's easy to lose sight of each other and of God. However, when you are both in the valley, the only thing that you can see is whatever is immediately in front of you, whoever is immediately beside you and what is immediately above you.

God can use a valley, however it is that you got there, to bring you closer to Him and to your spouse. The key is to not fight each other trying to claw your way out, but rather to work together. Sometimes we can be like crabs in a boiling pot of water. Although it is possible for one crab to claw his way out, his fellow crabs will never allow it because when he starts to make progress, they'll grab him and pull him back down.

There are exceptions, but in most cases, your spouse is not trying to ruin your life. Your spouse is not trying to make the wrong choices. They are not trying to make you and the entire family miserable. If they are, then that is an entirely different issue and we would recommend counseling. You are both essentially after the same goal. Don't allow the enemy to cause you to fight against your spouse in high-stress situations. As we noted earlier, changing your perspective can cause the tough seasons in life to bring you and your spouse closer together. It shouldn't be you against your spouse, but you and your spouse against the problem.

TAKE THE TIME

If we are taking the time to reconnect with our spouse in different ways, making it a point to avoid the things that may be deterring our spouse from being able to connect with us and trusting God with the realities of life beyond our control, we can build a marriage with an atmosphere of joy and peace, no matter what life throws our way.

WHAT WO/MEN WANT

#respect #security

culture • Men want meaningless sex and women want complete control
counter-culture • Men want to be respected and women want to be securely loved

two

WHAT WO/MEN WANT

What do women and men want? When faced with this question, we can legitimately respond with a myriad of answers ranging from the hottest new product on the market to our desire to be significant. Our responses may be different, yet still completely accurate. However, at our core we are created with one basic need - each one different for males and females.

Although we can be temporarily satisfied from the fulfillment of more superficial desires; in order for us to feel a more permanent sense of fulfillment, this basic need must be met. This explains why the vast majority of our behaviors can eventually be traced back to these needs. Understanding these needs, where they come from and how they affect our behavior is vital to the success of our marriages.

WHAT DO WE REALLY WANT?

If we were to take our notes from the culture we live in, the TV sitcoms and movies would tell us that wives want to be in charge and husbands want sex with no responsibilities. Although there seems to be truth to this on the surface, these things only bring temporary satisfaction and won't give us a deeply fulfilled life or marriage. In fact, we believe that if women are given an endless supply of unchallenged control, they will eventually feel unhappy and insecure. Likewise, if men are given an endless supply of meaningless sex and released from having any responsibilities, they will eventually feel disrespected and unsuccessful. Ironically, what men and women really need in order to feel deeply satisfied in their lives and marriages are precisely what is taken away from them when they are given what culture says they want.

At the core of their existence, men need to be respected – deeply admired, esteemed and honored for what they are able to accomplish. Another way of saying this is that men need to feel successful. Notice that it's not enough to simply be successful, he needs to feel successful. In order to feel successful, he not only has to be respected by those around him, but also respect himself.

Women, on the other hand, need to feel secure – confident that they are loved and cherished for who they are, protected from harm (spiritually, emotionally and physically) and free from fear and doubt. For women, it's not enough to be loved – she needs to feel secure in that love. It's not enough to never face challenges – she needs to know that there's someone who "has her back" when she does face challenges. It's not enough to be successful - she needs to feel secure of her value apart from what she can do.

In a nutshell, men need to feel successful by being respected for what they are able to do and women need to feel secure that they are loved and valued for who they are.

Given these wants and their definitions, it is easy to argue that they are interchangeable – that women want to feel respected as well and men also want to feel secure at times. It is true that every human wants to be respected and secure, and as we look deeper into these two wants, we are not denying that fact. However, we believe that a man's desire to be respected and a woman's desire to feel secure resonates more deeply with each respective gender.

For example, if a husband and a wife are both lied to, they will both feel hurt and offended. However, if you start digging into the core reasons why they feel hurt, you'll usually get slightly different answers. The wife may make a statement like "I can't trust him anymore", indicating that her security in that person has been damaged. Whereas a husband may make the statement, "How dare they lie to me", indicating that the husband believed he held more respect from that individual than for them to ever consider lying to them.

There are always exceptions to the rule, but in general, most people would agree with these statements. These gender-specific needs are not just eluded to in studies conducted by Dr. Emerson Eggerich,[1] but more importantly, founded in scripture.

Christ and the Church

> *"'For this reason a man shall leave his father and mother and be joined to his wife, and the two shall become one flesh.' This is a great mystery, but I speak concerning Christ and the church."*
> *–Ephesians 5:31-32 (NKJV)*

Biblically speaking, the husband represents Christ and the wife represents the church. Our marriages should reflect this same structure. Jesus Christ is our LORD and savior, not just our savior. Everyone wants a savior because that brings us security. Not many of us desire a LORD because that brings with it the idea of authority - but our relationship with Christ only flourishes when both these components are active in our lives.

> *"For God so loved the world that He gave His only begotten Son, that whoever believes in Him should not perish but have everlasting life."*
> *–John 3:16 (NKJV)*

> *"Whoever fears the Lord has a secure fortress…"*
> *–Proverbs 14:26 (NIV)*

God loved us so much that He provided for the world's most basic need by providing the security of salvation through Christ's death and resurrection. Once the world believes in and commits themselves to Christ, they receive that eternal security and become "the church". Being eternally secure is great for "the church" but in order to be fulfilled in our relationship with God, God wants us to give Him something in return – our respect as evident by your submission to Him. This submission to God is an act that communicates our trust in God's ability to successfully operate as our Lord and not just our Savior. Hence, in very basic terms, Christ provides the church with security because He loves us and the church gives Christ respect because He continuously proves His success as our Lord.

If we were to follow this example, a man would offer security and commitment through marriage. Once a woman accepts that offer, she becomes his wife. In order for their relationship to be fulfilling, the wife respects her husband by submitting to his authority, which communicates that she trusts her husband as a successful leader and not just as a contractual obligation. Simply put, ideally the husband would receive the respect he needs through his wife's willingness to submit and the wife would receive the security she needs through her husband's self-sacrificing love for her. Ideally.

As imperfect humans, we are severely flawed and so the analogy presented in scripture is not always carried out the way it should be. However, it does give us an example of what to work towards and a framework for how God intended marriages to operate. And as with all things that God communicates to us through scripture, what He asks of us may go against every fiber of our fleshly being, but ultimately, He created us and He knows what will bring us true joy and peace, even when it doesn't make sense initially.

WHAT WOMEN WANT: SECURITY

The first thing most people think of when they think of security in marriage is financial. Especially when it pertains to the husband's responsibilities in the marriage. The antiquated model showcases a husband who brings home the bread after a long day of work, kicks off his shoes and sits on the couch waiting for his wife to serve him dinner – satisfied that he has provided "security" for his family and thus, accomplished all that is necessary for him to accomplish as a husband and father.

However, providing security for your wife goes well beyond financial security. It may or may not even mandate that the male be the primary bread-winner of the family, although that is the generally accepted school of thought in today's culture. Biblically speaking, it is even possible for the wife to bring home most of the financial income and for the husband to still maintain his position as the head of the household and also provide complete security for his wife.

The need for a woman to feel secure is far less about being physically protected or financially provided for and far more to do with feeling loved without question, confident without doubt, cared for without being minimalized, valued without obligation, propelled without danger, encouraged without criticism and safe without limitations. The ability for a husband to provide security for his wife is a tall order and encompasses three parts: spiritual security, emotional security and physical security.

Spiritual Security

First and foremost, the single most important way that a man can provide the most security for his wife is by demonstrating that he loves God, puts his trust in God and is obedient to God. We say "demonstrating" these things to emphasize that not only must a husband actually love, trust and obey God, but his wife needs to see that he loves, trusts and obeys God through his lifestyle. So if a husband says he loves, trusts and obeys God, but behaves in such a way that contradicts God's character, he not only is NOT providing security but he is causing insecurity for his wife through the inconsistency in his words versus his actions.

When a wife is able to see that her husband, although flawed, genuinely loves God and desires to be obedient to God, she can feel secure in her marriage spiritually. This doesn't mean that her husband is perfect, or that he will always act Godly or that there won't ever be a wrong decision made, but it does ensure her that the compass that her husband is holding is pointing in the right direction and therefore, it's the direction that she can feel secure in following.

Emotional Security

Secondly, a husband provides security for his wife emotionally in two primary ways: proving that he is trustworthy and protecting his wife's heart.

The first part of this statement is fairly straightforward - a husband should never lie to his wife. She should be able to trust what he says. Even the smallest infractions can disrupt her security.

You may have seen or experienced an argument between a man and a woman where the man tells the woman a seemingly harmless lie and doesn't understand why the woman is so upset with him. The woman usually responds that "it's not about the lie, it's that you lied to me at all."

When something is said to be secure, you may think of a fortress with stone walls several feet wide and several stories tall. A fortress is supposed to be impenetrable. It provides its inhabitants with security because they can trust that nothing will tear down those walls and no one can come inside to harm them.

Likewise, a man's words need to be just as trustworthy – holding his wife at the center. She should feel that when her husband says something, there is nothing that will prove his words to be false and there is nothing hidden in those words that will later harm her physically or emotionally. By always being honest to his wife, a husband is providing her with the ultimate form of emotional security.

And just like a stone fortress, if her husband's words are ever found to be untrue, even once and no matter how unimportant, it will cause her to start questioning everything he says from that moment forward. Her once solid fortress will no longer feel as secure as it once did, she'll no longer trust it as strongly as she once did and consequently, won't respect it or admire it as much as she once did. A woman's respect and admiration for her husband flows out of her ability to feel secure with her husband. A husband who lies to his wife, not only hurts her ability to feel secure but he costs himself a large piece of the respect and admiration that he so desires from her.

So husbands, next time your wife asks you if you like her cooking, you may want to carefully consider your answer in light of what the truth means to her. How you answer and how she responds is an entirely different topic that we'll cover later in this book.

The second part of emotional security – protecting your wife's heart – is going to look different for each individual marriage. The only way to protect your wife's heart is to truly know and understand her at a level beyond what is required to maintain the superficial logistics of a marriage.

In our case, I (Gloria) am very sensitive when it comes to scary or sad movies. I can't even watch a movie trailer without it either completely freaking me out or tugging at my heart strings so much so that I dwell on that topic throughout my day. I guess you could say that I am easily moved by the emotional influence of a film – which would explain my passion for the power of movies.

Being aware of this sensitivity, Robert is able to be proactive in protecting me. Whenever he knows a trailer or advertisement is about to be shown that is going to rattle me emotionally, he gives me a warning so I can close my eyes and he mutes the TV so I can't hear it. It's such a small thing and some people might view it as silly, but it's said that "it's the small things that count." For me, this is one of the many small things that Robert does for me that makes me feel secure with him. It's just another reminder that he isn't only there to defend me when something is attacking me, but that he is also always on the lookout for anything that could cause me harm or distress.

In a way, he is modeling how God protects us. God not only defends us when the enemy finds his way onto our turf, but he also says that He "will go before you and make the rough places smooth" (Isaiah 45:2 NASB). That's what husbands should be doing for their wives. Always on alert, going ahead of their wives to protect her emotions.

Perhaps your wife doesn't have a sensitivity to certain movie trailers, but maybe whenever she gets around your mother she tenses up and says something she later beats herself up for. That's a perfect opportunity to be on alert when everyone is together and "save" her from saying something she'll regret later. Maybe your wife has a habit of overworking herself to the point of meltdown. That's a great opportunity to catch her before she gets to that point and insist she take a break of some sort. Perhaps your wife feels incredibly insecure in pursuing a new opportunity in life and you can provide her with the emotional security she needs by building up her confidence and supporting her.

How you protect your wife emotionally will be unique to what causes your wife emotional distress. If you don't know what causes your wife emotional distress, that might be a great conversation point. It's difficult to protect someone when you don't know what they are battling and a woman's emotions can be a very mysterious place. Communication is key.

Physical Security

Thirdly, a husband should protect his wife from physical threats. Thankfully, providing physical security is a much less mysterious task. From protecting her from being robbed in a dark alley to providing for her financially, making sure she knows that her husband will never leave her or protecting her from verbal threats - these are all ways to protect a wife physically.

For example, if a husband's mother or sister is verbally attacking his wife, it is his responsibility to protect her from that verbal abuse. The worst thing a husband can do in that situation is leave her to fend for herself – it shatters her ability to feel secure and trust that her husband will protect her. We're not saying to ever act disrespectfully. However, there are many respectful ways to let someone know that it's not OK to continue to attack your wife. Sometimes simply knowing that her husband is willing to stand up for her is enough.

Physical security can be protecting a wife from internal threats as well as outside threats. When I (Gloria) am working on a project, I find it incredibly difficult to interrupt my focus with something as negligible as eating. There has been more than one occasion that Robert has fixed me a meal and stood beside me while I sat at my computer, feeding me every bite of my dinner to make sure I'm staying alive. And as much as I hope he forgets every day, Robert also chases me down to take my vitamins – just as my dad did when I was a child. I mumble and complain almost every time he asks me if I've eaten or when I see those vitamins in his hand. But deep down, it makes me feel secure that I can trust Robert to protect me in those ways physically – even if my own negligence is the culprit.

Again, every marriage has its own unique dynamics. Knowing and communicating with your wife is the best way to understand how to provide physical security for her.

Security in God

Media in our culture has done a great job at selling us the idea that women do not want to be protected - that they can handle it completely on their own. Although it is true that many women are just as capable - if not more capable - of protecting themselves against physical attacks as their male counterparts, the debate is not whether women CAN protect themselves. The debate is whether or not a wife needs to feel secure that her husband is willing to sacrifice himself to protect her in order for a marriage to be successful.

What is portrayed in the media may be the reality for many women – that there is no one they can depend on except for themselves. This sadly leads to a very stressful and unfulfilled life for many of those women. Unfortunately, because these women lack other options, their viewpoints can't be easily dismissed.

Where a husband may fail to provide security for a wife, God is the ultimate provider. We must remember that wives are not to place their security in their husbands instead of God, but rather place their trust in their husbands as an act of submission to God. Ultimately, our trust must be in God Himself.

Women are strong. They can handle themselves if needed. But in a strong marriage, the idea is that they wouldn't be required to handle everything themselves. Ideally, they would be able to trust their husbands to protect them spiritually, emotionally and physically and have full confidence that their security is in good hands.

Self-Sacrifice

Christ sacrificed himself to provide security to the church – because it was in the best interest of the church, not in his best interest. What he had to go through was terrible, but he did it for the bride - the church. When husbands begin the pursuit of trying to protect their wives, it has to be in the wife's best interest, not the husbands.

We need to understand that the security provided by Christ was provided because of love. Simply providing security for your wife regardless of the reason, is not enough. There are many ways that husbands can provide "pseudo-security" because it is given out of a manipulative spirit. The goal is for husbands to provide true security for their wives because of their love for their wives - just like Christ provided security to the church because of God's love for mankind.

WHAT MEN WANT: RESPECT

Since we've spent so much time talking about how husbands can be better husbands, it's only fair that we switch gears and address how wives can be better wives. This is where it really starts getting scary. Let's be honest, it's almost become normal for the world to criticize a man on all the things he could be doing better. But start talking about all the different things that a woman could be doing differently? Now that's a different animal. Nevertheless, we shall tackle this beast and we pray that you (women) proceed with an open heart - and that you (men) will get rid of that smirk before your wife sees you.

Giving Admiration

We've already established that men ultimately desire respect to feel successful. But what are some ways that a wife can make her husband feel respected? Let's start with actually admiring her husband.

A wife should dwell on her husband's admirable qualities. This is where the wife is jokingly thinking.... 'what qualities?' Certainly there is at least one or two things that your husband does successfully. Let's be honest, you did marry him - and when you married him, you probably saw nothing but admirable qualities. In fact, your family and friends may have even done their best to point out all his flaws and yet you still chose to focus on all his admirable qualities and marry him anyway. More than likely, at least some of those admirable qualities still exist. Your perspective on those qualities may have changed, but they do exist.

One of the things that tends to frustrate me (Gloria) the most about Robert happens to be how easily frustrated he gets with the tiniest things and how when I do something frustrating, he calls me out on it. Whenever we get into an argument, these two tendencies always make their way to the surface – him getting frustrated at me for something and then calling me out on it because I should've known better.

What's interesting about these two things being the foundation of many of our arguments, is that those are the exact two qualities that attracted me to Robert in the first place. Robert and I met our senior year in high school on the side of a main road where all the wanna-be "fast and furious" drivers would cruise. They would blast their loud music and flash their stickered cars (ok, I was the only one with a stickered car, but I thought it was really cool). The following day, I saw Robert with a group of his friends and decided to attempt to be "cool" (something I was very far from actually being) and I casually made my way to him and asked "So. Hanging out in a parking lot. Is that actually all you do on a Friday night?" as if to say that it was a very uncool thing to do. With that comment, he gave me an "are you serious?" look and replied, "You were there too." Ouch. He totally called me out and from that moment on, I was hooked. I loved the idea that he was straightforward and confident and that he was willing to challenge me.

Fast-forward several years and he hasn't changed much in that aspect, but my perspective of those qualities has changed. I remembered that during one of our recent arguments. While Robert was getting frustrated, I decided to stop viewing it as something I disliked and just for a moment, pretend I was that high school girl getting called out by this (totally hot) guy I just met. And the strangest thing happened. All of a sudden, I wasn't mad at him anymore for calling me out, I was attracted to him for it. It was adorable.

I'm not saying that from that point on we never got in an argument about him getting frustrated too easily or challenging me. But what did happen is that I stopped dwelling on it as such a negative thing. Instead, I thought about the positive side of that personality trait. Yes, he gets frustrated and lets me know when I'm doing something dumb. On the other hand, he's successful in being totally honest with me and he successfully challenges me and he's not OK with letting me make a fool of myself - all qualities I admire greatly.

Focusing on your husband's admirable qualities doesn't mean that you put a blindfold over your eyes and deny that he has any areas of improvement. What it means is that you can acknowledge your spouse's weaknesses at the right time, without dwelling on them constantly.

Ultimately, you get to decide what you focus on. It's very likely that your spouse has an equal number of negative traits as they do positive traits - so why choose to dwell on, talk about and point out only the negative ones? Start dwelling on, talking about and pointing out the positive traits and you'll be amazed at how it changes your attitude towards your spouse.

Your husband desires to feel successful and admired, especially by his wife. The notion of a knight in shining armor may seem childish to you, but you would be hard-pressed to find a man that doesn't beam with the idea of having a wife that admires and adores him. He may know he has flaws, but not much can make a man feel more successful than a woman who chooses to downplay his flaws and spotlight the things he does right – in her heart and in public.

Giving Praise

This leads us to our next suggestion for how to make your husband feel respected by you. It's great if you've learned to admire your husband privately - but let's step it up a notch and make a diligent effort to praise him publicly – both are consistently necessary.

Imagine the effect it would have on your husband to hear you praise something about him or something that he did to a group of friends or colleagues. He would walk taller and with his head held higher. His confidence would sky-rocket. This doesn't just benefit the husband, but it benefits the wife. Because now, when he looks at his wife, he sees a woman that admires and praises him and makes him look good and in no way does he want to disappoint her. He'll have the fuel he needs to be the man she thinks he is and he'll do whatever he has to do to protect anyone from harming her.

Every time you, as the wife, compliment your husband, you are creating a bridge that your husband can cross to become more emotionally connected to you. If one of your complaints is that your husband seems to be emotionally disconnected, try a praise strategy and see if you don't get different results.

The key here is not to lie. We're not promoting complete disillusionment. It doesn't do you or your husband any good to go around praising him for things that don't even apply to him. "Death and life are in the power of the tongue" (Proverbs 18:21 NKJV), but that doesn't mean that your tongue is a magic wand that you can just speak and –POOF- it appears. It means that you have the power, through your words to build your husband up and remind him and yourself of all his great qualities so that he begins to believe in himself more and thus, feel more successful. At the same time, simply hearing yourself recite all your husband's positive traits will make those traits and the associated emotions more prominent in your mind. Even if you struggled to find good things to say about your husband initially, the more you verbalize those things, the more natural it will become.

The Opposite of Praise

Let's look at the other end of this. If every time you praise your husband he feels more successful, then what happens every time you critique, put-down or talk negatively about your husband?

If all you do is speak to your husband harshly, cut him down and tell everyone all the terrible and stupid things he does, then he'll feel like a failure and one of two things happen:

One route is that a man might turn his embarrassment into defensiveness and fabricate his own confidence, creating for himself an inflated ego. When this man looks at his wife, he doesn't care to protect her because she makes him feel like a failure. On top of that, his defensiveness and ego may turn him into a mean and harsh husband, who cares nothing about his wife's opinions or desires, making her feel unvalued and unloved.

On the other end of the spectrum, a man who is continually diminished by his wife's berating may start to believe her, hang his head in shame, be zapped of all confidence and feel worthless. This man may love his wife but doesn't have the confidence to protect her in any way even if he wanted to. This causes the wife to respect him even less and the cycle continues.

In both cases, the results are the same – neither husband receives the respect they need and so neither husband can nor are willing to give the wife the security and love that she needs. It's a terrible cycle which usually ends with both parties feeling unsatisfied in the marriage and wanting out.

Unfortunately, the only way to break this cycle is for one of the parties to recognize it and start reversing the cycle. That means, either the husband has to start loving his wife even if she doesn't act like she deserves it or the wife has to start respecting the husband even if he doesn't act like he deserves it.

That's always the hardest part – because nobody wants to provide something for someone when they deserve the exact opposite. But before you shut that idea down and say that you aren't going to be the one that starts repairing the cycle, let's remember that it's God's Grace that has forgiven you of every terrible thing you have ever done so that you could have the opportunity to not only experience the magnificence of Heaven, but to be seated by God as if you are treasured royalty. Do you think you deserve that type of treatment? If God can exchange your wrongdoings for such an incredible, massively undeserved gift, then perhaps you can find some way to do the same for your spouse.

Allowing Him to Lead

Lastly, one of the most prominent and difficult ways a wife can make her husband feel successful and respected is to allow her husband to lead the family. Before all the women start throwing darts, try to stick with us until Chapter 4 where we'll dive more into this concept.

For now, let's be open to the idea that allowing your husband to lead does not mean that you are weaker or less competent. It simply means that the roles and responsibilities that husbands are assigned by God, are different than the roles and responsibilities that are placed on the wife. Both positions are equally valuable and vital to the success of a marriage.

Part of allowing your husband to lead means not completely disregarding his opinions and not taking over and not assuming responsibility for everything your family does. Allowing him to lead means respecting his opinions, working with him on the best decision for the family and then ultimately allowing him the honor of making the final decision when you two do not see eye to eye on a topic.

We'll move on for now, but again, if you are appalled by this seemingly outdated idea, hear us out in Chapters 3 and 4 when we talk about those roles in more detail.

Respect is [NOT] Earned

There is an extremely common saying that "respect is earned, not given." People proclaim it as if it's the Bible (by the way – it's not) to justify treating someone disrespectfully. In fact, it's quite the opposite of how God commands us to treat others. 1 Peter 2:17 (NKJV) tells us to "honor all people. Love the brotherhood. Fear God. Honor the king." The verse doesn't say "Honor all people that deserve it" or "honor people [all being omitted]. The same is especially true when it comes to our spouses.

> *"However, each one of you also must love his wife as he loves himself,*
> *and the wife must respect her husband."*
> *–Ephesians 5:33 (NIV)*

It just doesn't get any more straightforward than that. There simply aren't many ways you can interpret "the wife must respect her husband". Respect is commanded, not earned.

If you are having trouble grasping such a concept, keep in mind, that most everything God commands us to do flies in the face of our fleshly knee-jerk reactions. But remember that He created us. He knows the actual psychology of how things work and if He tells you to do something, there's a reason.

More often than not, we have found that reason is not just spiritual, but it's also scientific and psychological. The more respect a wife gives her husband, the more confidence he will gain and the more respect he will deserve. So if you truly feel that your husband is not deserving of any respect, chances are pretty high that if you start respecting him, you'll create a husband who does deserve it.

Several years ago, we watched a popular TV drama that depicted this concept so beautifully. In this series, one of the main characters was a loathsome man. The writers spent a couple seasons making him one of the most lowly and disgusting humans that most any of us could imagine. In one of the later seasons of the show, this man conned his way (via murder) into a high-level position at a respected corporation. During his time there, he attended meetings, held seminars, etc. and he was highly respected by everyone that crossed his path. It was obvious that the first gesture of genuine respect he encountered at the corporation was a complete shock to him and the longer the respect continued, you could see his demeanor begin to transform. Receiving such a high amount of respect hit him where it counted and somewhere in his demented mind, he realized that this was the man he wanted to be – someone successful and worthy to be respected. Subsequently, when he was found out and was back on the run, he made a life-altering decision to release a family he was keeping as hostages. The decision was absolutely contrary to his character prior to his corporate experience. It was the experience of being successful and genuinely respected when he didn't deserve it that caused him to desire more of that respect and led him to make decisions that were respectable. I don't know if the writers of the show intended to communicate such a profound message, but that's certainly the message that was communicated to us.

THE CYCLE

Security and respect are both built on each other – in order for a husband to gain his wife's respect, she must feel secure and in order for a husband to be able to provide security for his wife, she must allow him to lead the relationship. The cycle must begin with someone somewhere. Regardless of whether or not your spouse is providing your basic need, start providing for theirs.

Let's bring it back to Christ and the church. The world needs the eternal security and love that Christ offers, but most people are not even aware of how badly they need it. They don't always accept what they need and they certainly don't usually give God what He created us for, but God continues to provide what we need anyway. Our marriages should model that same approach. We should continue providing what our spouse need from us whether they accept it or not, whether they deserve it or not, or whether they are providing for us or not.

Nothing melts the heart of a man more than the respect and admiration of his wife and nothing makes a woman respect and admire her husband more than to feel secure in his love and protection.

DICTATORS

#leadership

culture • Being the man of the house means ruling with an iron first
counter-culture • Being the man of the house means sacrificing as a servant-leader

three

DICTATORS
(from Robert)

When it comes to leadership, there are two flawed schools of thought roaming our society. The first error is one that has been made popular by modern sitcoms, novels and the occasional outspoken celebrities - that husbands are lazy and immature and wives are forced to take the leadership role in their marriage and families. The second error is one that has been popularized by religious circles that have misinterpreted what leadership truly is – it's the thinking that a husband who is the head of his house is a husband who lays down the law as a dictator and has a wife that is nothing more than a mere hired servant.

Neither one could be further from God's intention for the husband as a leader in his marriage and home. Like Jesus, God has called husbands to servant-leadership – a leadership style that requires a husband to love and serve his wife and family in such a way that he would give up his life for her; that he would become overwhelmingly uncomfortable if it meant the betterment of his wife.

THE STRUCTURE OF LEADERSHIP
Everyone, both male and female, is leading someone, somewhere. Leadership is influence. So much of what is written in this chapter can be

beneficial to anyone in any leadership capacity. With every opportunity to lead, there is a structure that needs to be established so that both the leader and those who are following are on the same page and can go the same direction. As creative and passionate as our God is, He is also a God of structure. It is the structure that God establishes that allows the fullness of life to flow at its highest output.

The same is true within our marriages. Our marriages are meant to be a vehicle that propels us further in our influence of those around us. However, when we operate outside of the structure that God has established in our marriages, we end up focusing on our inward turmoil and problems so much that we are not able to even think about influencing anyone in our world.

> *"But I want you to understand that the head of every man is Christ,*
> *the head of a wife is her husband, and the head of Christ is God."*
> *—1 Corinthians 11:3 (ESV)*

In every healthy organization there is a set infrastructure. Without knowing whose vision to follow, individuals cannot all work in unison to accomplish that vision. In 1 Corinthians, God makes his hierarchy clear: God is the head of Christ, Christ is the head of every man, and the husband is the head of his wife. Ultimately it is God's vision that we are created to follow and the method to follow that vision is through the infrastructure stated above. So, if this order offends you, please save the angry email. I didn't say it, God did.

A spiritual leader is a God-fearing, wife-cherishing, family-leading, Bible-believing, Holy Spirit-obeying, male head of the household. Now that may sound like a tall order or an unreachable goal but do not lose heart. This chapter should help you understand the process it will take to become that kind of leader. It doesn't happen overnight. However, it is on the husband's shoulder to properly lead his family in following the vision of God.

Now before every man in the room swells up with pride thinking that he can operate as the leader, independent of his wife's contribution, if we look further down this passage of scripture, we read:

> *"Nevertheless, in the Lord, woman is not independent of man nor man of woman; for as woman was made from man, so man is now born of woman. And all things are from God."*
> *-1 Corinthians 11:11-12 (ESV)*

Just as the Body of Christ are the arms and feet of Christ – carrying out the will of Christ, so the wife operates as a helpmate – in partnership with her husband in his pursuit of fulfilling God's vision for their lives with the husband at the helm. Without people that are willing to be led by Christ, Christ cannot accomplish what He has set out to accomplish. Without a wife's willingness to be led by her husband, the husband is incapable of accomplishing all that he is called to accomplish. Additionally, the church (or wife) will also never experience the greatness that God has in store for them either.

It is a mutual partnership. Both the husband and the wife are vital to the success of their marriage and fulfilling the vision of God for both their lives.

YOU ARE NOT A DICTATOR

A husband cannot independently rule the roost and operate on his own – with his wife operating as hired help - and succeed. He needs his wife's help in the areas that she is strong in order to succeed. The success of both parties is dependent on the other's fulfillment of their own role in the marriage.

Leadership is not a dictatorship. Dictators rule by force. You, the husband, cannot command your wife to submit to you. You cannot order your wife to do your bidding. You cannot force your way into God-approved leadership. Your wife has to come to the revelation of God's structure on her own. She has to choose to willingly follow you as you lead. Until she is willing to follow, you should continue to gently lead her with patience and love, while at the same time practicing the grace of Christ in times when she is not willing to follow.

> *"The husband provides leadership to his wife the way Christ does to His church, not by domineering but by cherishing."*
> *—Ephesians 5:23 (MSG)*

In order to lead your wife effectively, you must understand that Jesus led by enduring the torment of the cross for the people He led. He sacrificed everything He desired to fulfill God's vision of protecting His people.

Since God has placed you in a position of leadership over your wife, this doesn't mean that you are more valuable than she is or that you "get" to make all the decisions. It means that He is entrusting you – he is making you responsible - for the physical, emotional and spiritual well-being of His precious daughter.

If you are the father of a daughter, then you can only begin to comprehend the massive responsibility that you have just been given. You can also then imagine the greatness of God's wrath that may be produced if you, being responsible for His daughter's well-being, were to abuse your authority and cause any amount of harm to His beloved daughter.

Read Ephesians 5:23 again:

> *"The husband provides leadership to his wife the way Christ does to His church, not by domineering but by cherishing." (MSG)*

If God says you are commanded not to lead by domineering, then how are you to lead? By cherishing. Merriam-Webster defines "cherish" as "to hold dear: feel or show affection for; to keep or cultivate with care and affection." So you are to protect and love your wife as if your life depends on it. It's not that prized one-of-a-kind signed football encased in spotless glass sitting on the most prominent shelf in your house or the beautiful car you love so much that you should focus all your energy on cherishing. It's your wife that you should be placing on a pedestal, taking pride in and making every effort to ensure no blemish or injury befalls her.

The latter part of the definition of cherish is to "cultivate with care and affection." To cultivate something means to "improve or develop by careful attention" (Merriam-Webster). Hence, you can go even a step further and imagine that if you, being a father, had a daughter yourself, your concern is not only for her safety and well-being, but you would also want her to feel fulfilled in her life and you would want her to be able to utilize all her gifts and talents for the purpose they were given. That responsibility is on your shoulders, to make sure your wife is empowered by you to accomplish all that she feels God has called her to.

This is a heavy responsibility and a responsibility that God takes very seriously. So, before you go off spouting scripture about being the head of the household every time you and your wife get into an argument, take heed to remember all that your role encompasses.

LEADERSHIP IS SELFLESS

> *"Husbands, love your wives, just as Christ loved*
> *the church and gave himself up for her."*
> *–Ephesians 5:25 (NIV)*

If selfishness is being only concerned with one's own well-being and desires, then the exact opposite holds true for selflessness. Selflessness in marriage would be your willingness, as a leader, to sacrifice your own well-being and desires for your wife and family.

I think that most husbands would say that they'd be willing to die for their wife and children. But what if it wasn't the sacrifice of your existence that your wife and children needed? What if your wife needed you to sacrifice watching a major football game so you could spend some uninterrupted time reconnecting with her emotionally? What if she needed you to not spend that $1500 bonus check on a new big screen TV and instead, use it to buy a new washer and dryer set that keeps breaking down? Or maybe she needs you to sell that car you love so much to finance her dream of an education or a new business dream. What if your wife needs you to sacrifice your pride and get help for that addiction you keep holding onto so that she can feel secure in her marriage and your love for her? You may be willing to sacrifice your life, but are you willing to sacrifice less than your life for what your wife needs?

There is a story that Dr. Mark Rutland shares in his sermons that demonstrates this type of selfless leadership beautifully. In one of his countless counseling sessions, Dr. Rutland is counseling a husband and a wife who are at odds with their slew of various problems. As an example, the wife explains to Dr. Rutland that she is in desperate need of a new car. The car she currently drives constantly breaks down, leaving her and their three children stranded on the side of the road fairly regularly. Her husband has a nicer vehicle but uses it for his job so he can give a professional impression on his clients and employers. The wife understands that her husband needs a nice vehicle to feel successful in his career, so she's just asking for her own reliable vehicle. The husband then rebuttals and explains that he is trying to get her a new car. In order for the family to be in the best financial health, he feels that they do not need to get a loan on a new car, so they have been diligently saving up so that he can buy her a good car with cash. Besides, he is the head of the household and he is making a decision for the betterment of his family in the long-run and she should submit to his decision. With that, Dr. Rutland turns to the wife and explains to her that yes, her husband is the head of the household and she should respect his decision to buy a car with cash. The husband leans back in his chair and approvingly smirks. Then Dr. Rutland turns to the husband and tells him that as the leader of his household, it is his responsibility to make sacrifices in order to provide for the needs of his wife. If he is going to make the decision to save and buy a car with cash, then he also needs to make the sacrificial decision to give his wife the reliable car to drive their family around in and he needs to take the beat-up car.

This is what servant-leadership looks like. It's being able to make the decisions that are best for your family – both physically and spiritually – even if that means that the person who gets the blunt end of the stick is you, the husband. It's a position of constant sacrifice and constant dying to self. If the term "dying to self" sounds harsh, that's because it is. That is exactly what Christ did on the cross and exactly what Christ is asking us to do in our marriages as leaders.

If the cost of leadership seems like a price tag you aren't able to pay on your own, then you finally understand the magnitude of how important it is to be dependent on God to help you lead your family and how much you desperately need your wife to help guide you around the pitfalls that you may be blinded from.

Every man wants to be successful, because success brings with it, respect. The only way for you to be successful as a husband is for you to let go of your pride and be willing to submit yourself to God's authority.

LEADERSHIP IS NOT PRIDEFUL
Everybody wants to be "the boss." Because the boss is at the top of the totem pole. They are the ones that get to tell everyone else what to do. Unfortunately, most people in our culture equate boss with leader and they are two totally different roles.

Being a Boss
First, the word "boss" implies that someone is more important than someone else. But a leader, a good leader, is humble. They recognize that in order to achieve a common goal, the value of the people they are leading is just as high as the value of the person leading. After all, what good is a leader if there is no one to lead?

All political opinions aside, think of the foundational basics of America's democratic structure. The President is the leader of the nation. But who holds the power to appoint the President? Essentially, it's the people that he leads that give him permission to lead. He may hold the power to make decisions that affect everyone in the nation, but the decision and power to elect that person is with the people. The President should simply be executing a decision that is in accordance with the will of the people. It's a balance of power where two parties work together with two different sets of responsibilities to achieve a goal.

The same is true in marriage. A husband's position of leadership does not make him more important or more valuable than his wife. God places no greater value on a male than he does a female; no greater value on a husband than he does a wife. A male can accomplish nothing greater overall than what a female is capable of accomplishing. A male may be able to accomplish certain tasks "better" than a female but we must also remember that there are equally as many things that a female can accomplish "better" than a male.

God never intended for the wife to have to compete with her husband. He intended for the wife to complete the husband – to complement him. Women weren't created to do everything a man can do. Women were created to do everything a man can't do. The moment that you determine in your heart that your position of leadership means that what you can do is more valuable than what your wife can do, you have missed God's heart entirely. The issue should never be you against your wife. Instead, it is your wife and you facing life together.

> *"In the same way, you husbands must give honor to your wives. Treat your wife with understanding as you live together. She may be weaker than you are, but she is your equal partner in God's gift of new life. Treat her as you should so your prayers will not be hindered."*
> *—1 Peter 3:7 (NLT)*

Your wife is an equal partner in your marriage. On top of that, God even goes as far as to say that if you should treat your wife as if she is not your equal, your prayers are hindered. Wow. It's amazing to me that God puts such an emphasis on husbands and wives having equal value to Him that He institutes a cost to the misuse of your role should you treat her otherwise. The implication here is that your ability to walk in the full measure of victory and power of God is at stake if you abuse your power in your marriage.

SERVANT-LEADERSHIP

The second major difference between a boss and a leader is that a boss tells others what to do and being a leader does not mean that you get to delegate all tasks to others.

Leadership is not lazy. It doesn't mean that you get to prop your feet up on the ottoman with a remote control in your hand and order your wife to get you a drink. Servant-leadership calls you to recognize that your wife is exhausted and to use your authority to tell her to prop her feet up on the ottoman and you give her the remote and you get her water and you finish the dishes and you put the kids to bed. Also keep in mind that your opinion on her exhaustion is not as important as you might think. You don't get to assume that your wife has no reason to be worn out or exhausted. As servant-leaders, if she implies she's exhausted, we husbands must take that seriously and act accordingly. In order to be a good leader in your marriage requires you must lead with love and a servant attitude.

> *"Husbands, go all out in your love for your wives, exactly as*
> *Christ did for the church – a love marked by giving, not getting.*
> *Christ's love makes the church whole. His words evoke her beauty.*
> *Everything He does and says is designed to bring the best out of her,*
> *dressing her in dazzling white silk, radiant with holiness.*
> *And that is how husbands ought to love their wives."*
> *–Ephesians 5:24 (MSG)*

There just isn't anymore that I can add to that verse. If you skipped over it because it was indented and italicized, go back and read it. In fact, read it again anyway. It typically takes men a few times to hear something before they get it.

Your task as a leader is to "bring the best out of her" and to have your love "make her whole." This is one of Gloria's favorite verses concerning marriage. There simply isn't anything more romantic to her than the picture that God paints in this verse. As a servant-leader, everything you do should be out of love for your wife with an attitude to serve her. Remember, it's not always what you do, it's why you do what you do. Motives or perceived motives are extremely important. What motivates you to act is almost just as important as your actions.

To put this mildly - my wife can be emotional from time to time and many times, especially in my marriage, Gloria doesn't even know what she needs in those moments. In fact, what she needs may be very different than what she wants. There were times early in our marriage that she had a major meltdown and seemingly lost all sane control of herself. What she screamed she wanted was for me to leave her alone. But what she really needed was for me to take control of the situation, hold her and tell her everything will be OK. I don't hold some super-human power to read her mind. I only know this because when Gloria is sane, she has told me "Robert, if I ever freak out and meltdown, no matter what I say, what I really need is for you to take control of the situation, hold me and tell me everything is going to be OK."

In this case, I have to be able to discern what will really serve her better – leaving her alone to fight off a meltdown by herself as requested or being there for her despite her pushing me away. Just like submission doesn't mean my wife is my hired servant, being a servant-leader doesn't mean that I am my wife's hired servant. Hired servants are not empowered or given the authority to respond appropriately to the difference between what is requested and what is actually needed. Every marriage is different and every individual is different. You have to be able to communicate with your wife and your wife has to be able to communicate with you to determine what each party needs versus what is said fleetingly throughout the day or during an emotional situation.

REFUSING BITTERNESS

What becomes difficult in leading with love and a servant attitude is when your wife refuses to cooperate. As men, we desire to be successful and not much else makes us feel more unsuccessful as when we are trying to lead with love and serve our wives and they continue to disrespect us and fight for the authority in the family. It's even worse, if our wives sin in such a way that not only undermines God's expectations but also undermines you as a husband or your marriage as a whole. I believe this is why God specifically mentions the role of bitterness on our parts:

> *"Husbands, love your wives and do not be bitter toward them."*
> *–Colossians 3:19 (NKJV)*

That verse is not conditional and it doesn't use the terms "unless" or "only when". It is a command that applies in all cases. It is not in a human's natural make-up to want to be submitted to someone else. It is an easier choice for a Christian to submit their will to the Father's Will because He is perfect and all-knowing. It is far more difficult for a wife to submit to her husband because her husband is not perfect or all-knowing (I know guys, that one hurt). It is a process that God takes a wife through to realize and understand the benefits of submitting to her husband.

If you are "doing your part" and loving your wife to the best of your ability according to God's design and she still has not come around, it may be tempting to quit prematurely and grow bitter toward your wife for not following your lead. But be encouraged. It is during this process that it is crucial that you do not quit. Continue to show your wife love and a servant attitude and pray for her. Your faithfulness to God's Word will be the catalyst that changes your wife's heart.

SUBMITTED TO GOD

There is no amount of communication or counseling with your spouse that can replace what a genuine, intimate relationship with God can do for your marriage. I'm not talking about how much you pray for your marriage or how committed you are to going to church. I'm also not saying your marriage is dependent on your ability to lead a family Bible study every week or follow all of God's commandments flawlessly every day. What I am saying is that finding a real relationship with God is vital to your life on earth and eternally.

It is only God, through Jesus, who has the power to go beyond changing your behavior and actually transform your heart. The more you allow God to transform you into His image, the better husband and man you will become. The good news here is that no matter how difficult this role might sound, it comes with the greatest support plan of all time. The one who laid out the expectation is also the one that empowers us to live it out. However, this is only possible with an intimate relationship with Him.

I am not referring to religion and rule-following: praying every day, reading your Bible, going to church, not smoking/drinking/looking at porn, etc. - although all of those behaviors will eventually come in line with God's expectation as you grow closer to Him. But if you do only those things and don't have a real relationship with God, then you could become an overbearing legalist. Besides, doing those things in your own effort is like winding up a ticking time bomb. Eventually it will go off because the flesh is simply not capable of overcoming the flesh. We require Christ.

What is needed is a genuine love for God - not just for the things of God but a love for God Himself. This love is proven and demonstrated by your desire to have an intimate relationship with Him.

Imagine a picture-perfect relationship with your children. Is it a relationship where the child follows all your rules? What about if they follow all your rules but never speak to you unless they are asking for something they want? Or if they follow all your rules but never speak to you, don't really know anything about you and don't care to be around you or care about you personally? Would that be your ideal relationship with your children? If your children grow up to be estranged from you but are individuals that follow all the rules and are successful in life, why isn't that enough for you for an "ideal" parent-child relationship? What's missing?

It's the relationship aspect that's missing. I'm sure as parents you would be happy that your children grew up to be successful, but every parent that I have ever come across desires a personal relationship with their kids. They love and care about their children and want their children to return that love. Most parents desire for their adult children to want to spend time with them and talk to them without ulterior motives.

If that holds true for earthly parent-child relationships, why wouldn't that hold true for our spiritual Father-child relationship? God doesn't just desire for you to keep all His commandments and be successful in your life and yet be estranged from Him. He desires real relationship. God desires to walk with you and talk to you. He desires for you to love Him, to want to spend time with Him and hear His voice.

It's through this type of relationship that you can submit yourself to God. It's when you understand His love for you that you are able to trust Him to lead you in all aspects of your life. It's through your submission to God that you can not only lead by example but also help your wife to be able to place her trust in you. As you allow God to lead you, she will be more willing to let you lead her.

"And He said to him, 'you shall love the Lord God with all your heart,
and with all your soul, and with all your mind.'"
–Matthew 22:37 (NASB)

ESTABLISHING GOD IN YOUR HOME

Once God is established in your life, the next phase is to lead your family in establishing God in your home. This can look different for each family.

However you choose to establish God in your home, the end result must be that you are making God's truth and wisdom evident outside of the four walls of the church. Whether it's through structured study of the Word, regular family prayer-time, regularly discussing the Biblical-view of situations or conversations throughout the day. There are many ways to ensure that your relationship with God is passed down to your family.

What I do want to clarify is that this doesn't mean you have to become "super-spiritual weirdos". Many people, especially men, have a "go big or go home" mentality. They think that if they can't read the Word and pray for two hours a day or if they don't know how or can't lead a family-based Bible-study every week, that there isn't any point in trying. Start where you are with something that is a small step in the right direction. Praying the Lord's prayer with your children before bed is an incredible step in the right direction. In his book, "21 Seconds to Change Your World", Dr. Mark Rutland estimates that it only takes twenty-one seconds to say the Lord's prayer.[1] That twenty-one seconds a day could change your life and your family's life.

The point is not to establish a tyrannical, rigid, old-school religious household. The point is to bring God's love into the house and into everyday conversations with your family. You don't have to get weird with it, but you don't want talking about God or showing love to be unusual in your house either.

BE YOUR WIFE'S SERVANT-LEADER

As a servant-leader, your primary responsibility is to protect your wife and family from spiritual, mental, emotional and physical damage. This requires a balance between standing up strongly for what your family needs and serving humbly to guide them in the right direction. Keep in mind that people, especially women, are more easily moved in your direction when pampered with love than when forced with presumptive authority.

Several years ago, Gloria and I got into a massive fight. She absolutely refused to do anything I asked her to do. She treated me poorly and continued to disrespect me the remainder of the evening. I don't even remember what she was so upset about (which isn't unusual), but my guess would be that she was just in a bad mood that day (she'll admit to that if you ask her). Typically, I don't have the patience to deal with those types of situations, but this time around, I decided to try a different approach to the argument. Instead of arguing back when she was obviously no longer thinking logically, I decided to serve her. In the midst of her insults and stomping around, I cleaned up the house, put the kids to bed, cooked her dinner in bed alongside a note of appreciation and a flower, brought her water and Tylenol, fixed the bed for her, put on some soothing music and asked her if there was anything else she needed. She didn't break right away, but after several minutes of letting the situation soak in, she ended up apologizing. It was a shock to me. If I would've tried to "win" the argument, she would have fought back harder and the situation would've escalated. But she says it was my serving her even in the midst of hostility that softened her heart and made her realize how wrong she was for treating me the way she did.

Pastor Robert Morris once that God spoke to him during an argument and asked "Do you want to be right or do you want to be right with".[2] Right with who? Right with your wife and right with God. Remember, what is your motivation. Are you motivated to be right or are you motivated by love for your wife? Dying to self often means we give up our goals of being right for the more rewarding goal of being "right with".

In that scenario, I was able to protect Gloria from further emotional damage by humbling myself and serving her - even when I wasn't the one that needed to apologize for anything. We men think that it's our brute strength that makes us suitable protectors. Although our physical strength has advantages in protecting our families, most of the time it's our willingness to let go of our pride and become servants for our families that has the most power in protecting our families.

IT'S OK TO ADMIT WEAKNESSES

Don't be afraid to delegate. Earlier in this chapter I said that being a leader doesn't mean delegating all your tasks to your wife. Being a leader also doesn't mean taking on responsibilities that you know you aren't good at. Your wife is your helpmate. It's a partnership. If there are areas that she is better at than you, then it's ok to ask her to handle that part of your life. Again, what the husband handles and what the wife handles is going to differ for every marriage depending on which spouse is better at which tasks.

RAISE YOUR WIFE'S SELF-ESTEEM

I know that this is going to come as a shock to you, but I have been told that most women are deeply insecure.[3] Even the women that appear confident and "put-together" have a high-level of insecurity. Something about how they are built. Knowing this makes their need for security in marriage and life make even more sense.

With that said, many women may never feel as though they are able to believe in themselves or reach their potential without a push or encouragement from someone else. There may be many people and mentors that can pour encouragement into your wife's life, but none of it will mean half as much as having the encouragement and support from her husband. When you, as her husband, are able to recognize her skills and talents and encourage her to pursue her dreams, it builds her up to a level that is unmatched.

HOW TO BE MARRIED TO A SERVANT-LEADER

Gloria will go over these statements in more detail in the next chapter, but just as an overview, here are some suggestions if you find yourself in a situation where your husband is not stepping up to the plate as a servant-leader.

First, let him lead. This may sound obvious to you, but your husband cannot have the opportunity to lead if the position isn't vacated. If you want your husband to be a leader, you have to step out of that role without trying to take over the minute you feel like he may make a wrong decision.

Secondly, build his confidence. If your husband lacks the confidence or know how to lead effectively, lovingly encourage him to take the lead. You'll be amazed at how much a man can accomplish when there is a woman (who isn't his mother) who believes in him.

Third, be his helpmate. Once you've vacated the leadership position and built his confidence up to attempt to lead, don't just leave him hanging out to dry. God created you to be a helpmate, so if there is a tough decision that needs to be made, provide your input and suggestions. Telling your husband what decision you would make, doesn't mean that he didn't make the final decision. Tell him your opinions and then let him know that you support whatever decision he makes - and then (here's a big one) actually support whatever decision he makes.

This brings us to the last point. Downplay the failures. I know this seems counter-productive. But in most cases, if your husband makes the wrong decision, he knows it. He may not admit it or want to talk about it, but he already knows it. The last thing he needs is for his wife to rub it in. This only serves to tear him down. If he fails, don't remind him, just build him back up to try to lead again.

As a wife, you are the best help that God could create outside of Himself. Recognize where your husband needs help according to God's structure for marriage and assist your husband in those areas. He may be called to lead the family, but He can't lead without you.

DOORMATS

#submission

four

DOORMATS
(from Gloria)

If you are anything like me and tend to judge a book by its most interesting or controversial topic, then you may have landed yourself in this chapter before reading the previous chapter on leadership. This is a tough chapter. It addresses concepts and ideas that the majority of modern women will immediately reject - especially if read out of context. However, before rejecting this chapter altogether, I implore you to make sure you've read the previous chapter (Chapter 3: Dictators), as the idea of female submission is much more easily understood when we are aware of what type of leadership God has intended us to be submitted to.

Submission. It's amazing how one word can evoke a diversity of emotions, opinions and perspectives. From my (Gloria) experience, when the typical modern woman hears that word, something in her immediately gets defensive – sometimes violently defensive. I know because I was no different.

From as early as I can remember, I have been the most independent, "strong-willed" and disrespectfully outspoken female you could meet. There was no person or authoritative position that I hesitated to stand up against. Submitting to legal and workplace authority was a serious struggle for me - so submitting to a husband who was supposed to be my equal was totally absurd.

Robert and I got married at the ripe, young age of 19, I remember when we attended our premarital counseling sessions. It was obvious that we had thought our relationship and our future through and were not just young kids getting married on a whim. Everything seemed to be progressing well until the counselor started discussing the concept of a submissive wife with me. I wasn't having it. I thought the guy obviously lived in the dark ages and if he thought for one second that I was going to be some doormat and let my husband do whatever he wanted to do, he was out of his senile mind. Needless to say, I made it very clear that the guy obviously did not know what he was talking about and we never went back to finish our counseling.

I know this can be an extremely difficult topic for women. I am not a naturally sweet, soft-spoken conservative girl who's "Leave it to Beaver" mother taught her how to cook from scratch and never to question her elders. To submit (to anyone) is a battle that fights against every fiber of my flesh. Although my opinion of submission has completely changed, it is still not something that comes naturally. This chapter is as much for me as it is for every wife out there.

It is only through God's revelation (and irony) that a girl whose biggest "flaw" was submitting to authority is now one of the biggest advocates of respecting authority and this includes the role of the "submissive wife." Oh, if only all my past teachers, bosses, counselors and friends could hear me say that – they'd be shocked. As I continue to explain the revelation that God gave me, my prayer is that you would be willing to have an open mind and consider honestly the argument for submission that is presented in the remainder of this chapter.

On the extreme opposite end of the spectrum, if you are a woman who has taken on the role of a submissive wife and have interpreted "submissive" to mean that you are to clean, cook, pop-out babies and do as your told, then I pray that this chapter will help you to step into the stronger role as the woman and wife that God has called you to be.

WHAT IS SUBMISSION?

"Wives, be subject (be submissive and adapt yourselves)
to your own husbands as [a service] to the Lord."
–Ephesians 5:22 (AMP)

The word "submit" in these verses is the Greek word, "hypotasso", which means to "arrange under".[1] You'll see in the definition of "hypotasso", that what it does not say is that the "submissive" party is weaker, less competent, less important or has a less impactful role.

In a perfect world where nobody disagrees, it's a grand idea to say you and your husband get "equal" input and make decisions "equally". But let's be real. There are many times that you and your husband probably do not agree. So who really gets to make the final decision? My observation is that in a relationship where leadership/submission roles are not established, the spouse that is the loudest and most persistent gets the final say. So is it truly "equal" or is every decision simply made by the person who out-fights the other?

Every partnership has to have a tie-breaker. A system set in place to decide who gets to make the final decision if the parties can't seem to agree. Fortunately, we need not worry about how that is supposed to take place in our marriage. God has set a standard. He has commanded that the wives "arrange" themselves under their husbands and to support them in unity.

THE ARGUMENT FOR SUBMISSION

In order for you to be truly united as a married couple, one of you HAS to be willing to arrange yourselves in unity under your spouse - and it is the wife who gets the privilege of being the support system that keeps the house from crumbling. Still not convinced you really buy into the idea of a submissive wife? There's plenty of other ways to look at the argument for submission.

Not Wired for Stress

We, women, make me laugh sometimes – our irony. We insist on doing everything ourselves and making all of our own decisions, because we think we know what will make us happy. But look at the state of women in today's society - one in four women are prescribed a mental health medication with anti-depressants being the most commonly utilized of these drugs.[2] We're depressed, anxious and stressed-out. We're overwhelmed and yet we refuse to let someone take the reins. We tell ourselves we can handle it - but then we find ourselves curled up in the corner of the bathroom crying our eyes out on the verge of quitting everything (or maybe that was just me.)

NEWS FLASH. We were not created to "handle it" ourselves. We were not wired to be able to carry the emotional burden of logistically doing everything, emotionally pouring ourselves out and then to also carry the burden of making every major decision in our lives.

Marriage is a life-jacket for a woman's emotional sanity. It's not a one-man show. If it were, why did you get married? If you could run everything yourself, then why not stay single and do as you wish with your life and make your own decisions? Marriage is a union ordained by God to help you and your spouse to change the world around you more effectively than if you were single. And if that's the case, then there must be some benefit, beyond simply having a companion, that God had in mind when He decided how marriage would be structured.

What if one of the major benefits of marriage is to take some of the stresses that women innately tend to consume themselves with and place it on the husband, who may be more able to deal with those stresses because he doesn't tend to allow himself to get carried away emotionally? Most women tend to over think and over analyze everything and sometimes we need to be able to trust someone else to make the decision for us. Perhaps submitting to your husband is God's way of protecting you from yourself – but you have to be willing to do it before you can start to see the benefits.

If not for your Husband, then for God

If you aren't really the type of woman who finds yourself stressed and overwhelmed, then here's a completely different perspective to the submission argument. Read Ephesians 5:22 again.

> *"Wives, be subject (be submissive and adapt yourselves)*
> *to your own husbands as [a service] to the Lord."*
> *–Ephesians 5:22 (AMP)*

It's almost as if God is saying "as a favor to Me, adjust your attitude and support your husband for your husband's benefit." Perhaps God is acknowledging that husbands need a tremendous amount of help and support and even if they don't know it or deserve your support, because you are obedient to God, you should willingly submit to your husband. At the end of the day, being a submissive wife is not just for your husband's benefit, it's also for yours.

I have found, from personal experience and observation, that women who have a problem submitting to their husbands also have a problem submitting to other authority that they strongly disagree with. At the top of that authoritative totem pole is God. If you, as a wife, refuse to submit to your husband, then you are refusing to submit to God, and that's only going to hold you back from having joy and peace in all facets of your life.

Submission is a Command

Whether we feel like living our lives stressed-out and "on our own" or not, if our desire is to live our lives for Jesus, then that means obeying His commands. If we are adamantly against the idea of submitting to our husbands, then that means that somehow, we have determined that submission is an option. The idea that submission is a choice, is a gross misconception. Submission is a command. It's not a preference, feeling or suggestion. That's a difficult statement to swallow (for me at least).

Just because I don't like the idea of submission, or just because it doesn't line up with my philosophy of woman empowerment, or just because it makes me feel like I'm giving up and I'm weak, doesn't mean that the rule doesn't apply to me...or you. Because culture has migrated away from the idea of submission or put a negative spin on it, doesn't make it less applicable. We cannot pick apart the Bible and only carry around the scriptures we like and then pretend the scriptures we do not like, do not exist. It simply doesn't work like that.

On an even deeper note, if you call yourself a Christian and say that Jesus is the Lord of your life - meaning He rules your life and you submit to His will – then by not submitting to your husband, you are living in disobedience to God. It is through obedience that we grow closer to God and He takes us further into the destiny and purpose that He has for our lives. So in the end, you may be sacrificing your own destiny if you continue to rebel against the concept of submission. This is not meant to be an indictment, it's simply meant to bring awareness to the seriousness of the issue. It's meant to provide an opportunity for us (women and wives) to examine ourselves.

Change is a Process

In a marriage where both the [servant] leadership role (as described in Chapter 3) and the submission role are established, submission is easier for the most part. It's not so much of a struggle for a wife to submit to a husband that has proven that he is a servant-leader, consistently sacrificing what he desires and making God-submitted decisions that he genuinely believes are best for his family. In this type of marriage, the wife feels confident and secure in her husband and therefore feels safe in submitting to his authority.

But most marriages don't start out this way. Mine sure didn't. The first few years of our marriage, it was a constant power struggle – trying to make decisions "equally" but ending up giving the decision-making power to the last one standing. I (Gloria) was bound and determined not to let Robert make a decision that I felt was not the right decision. I wasn't the only one struggling with my "role". During those years, Robert had a very expensive car hobby and a love for the latest electronic devices, which didn't fit well with the income-level of two poor college kids. Needless to say, Robert struggled with the "servant" part of leadership and making decisions that were best for the family. So, what then? Was I excused from allowing him the privilege of having the final say? Was his inability to make wise decisions or be self-sacrificing in his leadership style enough for me to be justified in my unwillingness to be a submissive wife? Unfortunately, no.

The requirement for submission is not void just because the husband is not fulfilling his role correctly. If your marriage isn't operating in the ideal servant-leader/submission structure yet, there is a process to get there. Sometimes it's a difficult process. Much of learning how to be a submissive wife or a spiritual leader is revelation and transformation that only God can take you through via prayer and a willing heart. It's the process of becoming spiritually mature. The problem is, in many cases, both spouses are not on the same spiritual journey at the same time. Sometimes, it's one spouse that gets a revelation and is called to start practicing obedience in their marital role before the other spouse cares to join them on that journey. This means that the spouse who chooses to submit to God first must trust God to change their spouse's heart and continue to walk in obedience regardless of their spouse's actions. This will be an especially challenging season but it is the very definition of faith. "Faith is the substance of things hoped for, the evidence of things not seen" (Hebrew 11:1 KJV). This is an exemplary situation of when your faith should be exercised. You must step out in obedience with faith that God will pull it all together, even when the evidence of your situation tells you that your family will not be able to withstand the results of poor decision-making.

After all, what's your other option? To continue to walk in disobedience, while your spouse also walks in disobedience? Two wrongs don't make a right. In the spiritual realm, at least one person, has to be walking in obedience and praying in order for God to start doing a work in that particular situation. It has to start with someone and if your spouse hasn't received the revelation of their role in the marriage yet, then the burden of starting the process is on you.

MISCONCEPTIONS OF SUBMISSION

Let's say that you've come this far in the book and are willing to explore this idea of submission further, but there's still a lot of preconceived notions about being a submissive wife that don't sit well with you. There are several misconceptions surrounding the idea of submission. I don't know that we can cover them all, but we can definitely dive into some of the more prominent ones.

Submission can't be Forced

You can't make your spouse fulfill their role in the marriage, just like they can't make you fulfill yours. We have all heard the scenario: A husband and wife are in a heated argument and the husband finally blurts out "Don't you read the Bible, you have to submit, I'm the head of this household!" While what he is saying is true, he's wrong (dangerously wrong) in his approach – and very well could suffer hazardous dangers to his health by making such a comment. Submission must be done willingly. We, wives, have to choose to actively submit. It cannot be forced on us. Reading Colossians 3:18-19 again:

> *"Wives, submit to your own husbands, as is fitting in the Lord. Husbands, love your wives and do not be bitter toward them."*
> *–Colossians 3:18-19 (NKJV)*

What this verse does not say, is "Husbands, make your wives submit to you, as is fitting in the Lord." It is not in God's character to force anyone into relationship with Him or obedience to Him. Instead, God continues to love mankind and waits patiently to be invited into their lives. As we covered earlier in the book, a husband is representative of Christ and the wife is representative of the church. So as the husband reflects Jesus and

His character, he should also understand that his wife has to be willing to actively submit to him. Women should never be forced to submit outside of their willingness to do so.

But What if He's Wrong?!?

Ultimately, choosing to submit to your husband in obedience to God means you are trusting God, even if you don't necessarily trust your husband. Most of the time, the whole submission concept scares women because we're so afraid that if we let our husbands start making the final decision, that even with our very rational arguments, they'll make decisions that will ruin our lives. Yes, there may be some decisions that cause consequences that will affect the whole family for a season. That's part of the burden for the man as he learns to lead. But we women need to let go of the idea that everything in life must be perfect and accept that when it comes to submission, it is OK for some battles to be lost so that the war for your marriage and family can be won.

You may be right about a certain decision. Your husband may be way off-course and he may not be seeking God as much as you are as to what direction to go. You have two options:

The First Option: Demand or push for your way and destroy the opportunity he has to learn to be a leader. By doing this, you also diminish any chance for him to learn from experience how to truly respect and value your opinions. On top of that, you destroy his confidence in himself to make decisions and lead his family or you give him reason to build a wall of bitterness. The lack of confidence or the wall of bitterness may prevent him from stepping out on the job or into what God has called Him to do. On your end, you just picked up the burden of that decision and stressed yourself out fighting about it and caused a lot of unneeded strife in your home. In the long-run, this scenario ends badly for everyone – you're too stressed to actually pursue what God has for you, your husband has low self-esteem and can't follow what God has for him, your marriage is full of tension and strife and your kids don't experience a peaceful home. Instead, they grow up watching their parents fight rather than seeking God and following Him in obedience.

OR

The Second Option: Even though you know that he is making the wrong decision, after you've made your argument [respectfully], you say "I don't think that decision is a good idea, but if you really feel that it's best for the family, then I'll support you and help you make it happen." First, he's SHOCKED, then his confidence skyrockets because he has a wife that trusts and respects him enough to follow his lead. When he no longer has to "fight" to get his way, he either realizes that he doesn't really want to make the wrong decision – especially now that you are putting the responsibility of that decision into his hands or he goes through with that wrong decision. Then after he learns that he made the wrong decision (and you didn't rub it in with "I told you so's"), he realizes that leading the family and "getting" to make the final decisions is a burden that he cannot bear all on his own. With this revelation, your husband starts to depend more on God to help him lead, he learns that he really should value your opinion much more than he did and he'll make better decisions the next time. Even though the entire family has to endure a less than ideal season because of a bad decision, that season will pass. God is still in control and He honors your willingness to be obedient to Him and continues to bless you regardless of your husband's bad decision. On top of all that, your children get to witness the exchange of love, respect and humility within your marriage that they can carry into their own lives.

Not every scenario will work out exactly like the two options above. But in general, they tend to run along these lines. You could win the battle with the first option and lose the war or you could lose the battle with the second option but win the war.

Even in writing this chapter, Robert cut many statements out that he said were ramblings. I didn't necessarily agree. I wrote them because I thought it contributed to the point. But at the end of the day, I don't have to break a sweat about it. I trust that Robert and I have both poured ourselves out in prayer over the words in this book and if God felt that something was absolutely necessary to drive a point home in this chapter, then I'm confident that God would have directed Robert to keep those "ramblings" in here. If Robert's wrong, I trust that God will still work it out for the benefit of His Kingdom in the end. On the other hand, I do tend to ramble, so perhaps he did you (our readers) a huge favor and you should applaud the leadership/submission structure in our marriage because it probably saved you much cringe-worthy reading.

At the end of the day, if you cannot trust that God - the creator of the entire universe, the Alpha and Omega, the One who can see the beginning to the end and everything in-between – might know what He is doing, then who can you trust? What He says may seem contrary to your existence, it may not make logical or emotional sense, but being obedient to God always takes you where you want to be – physically and emotionally.

You are not a Hired Servant

This is where we get the chapter title "doormat". If I had to choose the biggest misconception about submission, it would be this one – that submission means you are an SWB – servant with benefits (yes, I made that acronym up). This is the misconception that says that a "submissive wife" is a wife that cooks, cleans, pops out babies and has sex with her husband on demand, but otherwise relinquishes her right to an opinion of any and all decisions in life.

Submission does not mean that you disown your voice and when your husband calls for water, you jump up and get it, bringing it back to him with your head bowed. That's a servant or a slave, not a submissive wife.

When God created woman, it was to "make him a helper suitable for him [man]" (Gen 2:18 NKJV). Adam already had charge of all the animals of the earth, he didn't need another creature he could order around. In fact, it is a woman's voice and guidance that makes her an invaluable "helper" for her husband. A wife that holds her tongue in regards to her opinions and insight in an effort to be a submissive wife is actually doing her husband harm and not helping at all. A "yes [wo]man" doesn't help a leader lead, it hinders a leader's ability to lead because it leaves that leader to make potentially harmful decisions based on his own limited thoughts and knowledge.

God did not put women on the earth to be silenced in a corner, God put women on the earth to partner with their husbands and help them lead the families to change their worlds. A wife simply cannot do that if she is not given the opportunity to speak to her husband as an equal.

Submission does not mean that you are less than your husband. You are equally competent and equally valuable. In fact, it's the quality of your competence and foresight that makes you the helper that God intended you to be.

Let's breakdown what God is really saying in Genesis 2:18 – "…make him a helper suitable for him." So, we know that there are two different goals that God was trying to accomplish when He created a woman:

First, she's a helper – someone who's job is to help her husband. The Hebrew word used here for "help" is "ezer"[3] - which is the same word used to define God in His role in helping mankind in Psalm 33:20, Hosea 13:9 as well as many others. So before anyone starts thinking that a helper is someone who is less competent than the person needing help, let's remember that it's God who also helps mankind. This is such an incredible thought. The creator of the universe and our Lord practices the very same form of "help" that He intended the woman to offer her husband. Being a helper means that you have something that can assist someone else and you are generous and gracious enough to allow that someone else to benefit from you.

Then God states that the woman is to be "suitable for him." The Hebrew word for "suitable" is "neged" which is defined using words like "parallel", "corresponding to", "in front of" and "counterpart".[4] These words not only describe physical proximity, but also mental proximity. Meaning, a wife is someone of equal merit or comparable to her husband. For example, a wife can be comparable to her husband in intelligence so she can challenge the way he thinks with credible arguments.

In Genesis 33:12, the word "suitable" is used in another way - "Then Esau said, 'Let us journey on our way, and I will go AHEAD [neged] of you.'" Esau offered to go ahead so that he could pave the way or warn those following him about any potential dangers.

So when God says a wife is a "helper, suitable for him", we get a picture of a woman who is wise, perhaps has greater spiritual sensitivity than her husband and is able to think of things ahead of time to help her husband avoid pitfalls of potentially foolish decisions. Most people would agree that these are innate characteristics of most women. It's these characteristics that make us "more competent" in many ways and we are to use these skills to assist our husbands in leading our families on the right path.

Our husbands should be aware that God has given them wives to keep them from making foolish decisions and wives should be aware that God has commanded us to follow our husband's lead so that we do not have to suffer the emotional burdens that come from having to carry all the weight of our family's well-being ourselves.

It's a beautiful partnership of a husband and wife hand-in-hand whose hearts are submitted to each other. This is the relationship that God has intended for the structure of our marriages. Submission is not the end of your independence, it's the vehicle to your strength!

Submissive Wife does not mean Stay-At-Home Wife

The other day I watched a disturbing video (disturbing to me anyway). It was a video of a very elderly lady going on a long rant about the women of today and how a "woman's place is in the home - to raise her children and feed her husband." I couldn't help but think to myself that that is exactly what society thinks of when someone says "submissive wife" and it couldn't be more wrong.

Being a stay-at-home mom or wife is a career choice, not necessarily an act of submission. There are plenty of women who choose to stay-at-home and yet would not be considered submissive wives by anyone's definition.

If that's the career that a wife chooses and feels called to, then that's a good and fulfilling calling. However, for someone to say that a wife is not submissive if she works outside the home is simply not Biblical.

If you are wondering what type of woman God considers "virtuous", there is no need to look any further than Proverbs 31. There is so much in Proverbs 31 that we could dive into, but we'll try to stay on topic. I encourage you to read and study the chapter in its entirety.

In Proverbs 31, the virtuous wife is described as a wife who "...considers a field and buys it; from her profits she plants a vineyard...She perceives that her merchandise is good...(NKJV)." Among all the many things she does to provide for her family's needs, this woman also handles business transactions and investments. She has her own business - her own career outside of the home.

This woman speaks my language. I'm an ambitiously career-driven woman. Business-minded with huge God-sized dreams. It's not every woman's desire to be at the top of a corporate ladder, but if it is something you feel called to, I hope Proverbs 31 releases you to do so. If nothing else, she clarifies that being a submissive wife does not mean that you have to choose between being a stay-at-home wife/mom or pursuing a career. In my opinion, neither of those options are better than the other. What's most important and "better" is doing what you feel God has called you to do.

The key point that I had to learn in my pursuit of having it all (family, children, career) is that pursuing my career is out of order if my family begins to be neglected. If I'm working on a major project, I tend to become a workaholic. I don't know when to stop and that's certainly not Biblical either. God is a God of balance and seasons. As women, we have a tendency to take on too much and we need to learn to set boundaries for ourselves and allow different seasons in our lives to take precedence if needed.

This is where the "submissive wife" role is a life-saver for me. When I get carried away and my family and my health starts suffering, Robert steps in. He firmly reminds me of my priorities and the need to be balanced and he pulls me back to sanity. If I did not respect his leadership and he tried to pull me out of my workaholic state, I have no doubt that a massive fight would break out and I'd continue to bulldoze my way through my work. It's only because the leadership/submission structure is well-established that my submission worked out to our benefit.

I'd like to think that, like Proverbs 31 implies, women can have and do it all. I've also learned, that in order for that to happen, there has to be someone in our lives that holds the reins and protects us from ourselves. If you are so focused on not being submitted to your husband, you could be rejecting what you need - to have the physical and emotional stamina to do everything you are called to do.

HOW TO SUBMIT

> *"Now the Lord God said, 'It is not good (sufficient, satisfactory)*
> *that the man should be alone; I will make him a helper*
> *(suitable, adapted, complementary) for him."*
> *—Genesis 2:18 (AMP)*

Up until this point, we've spent the chapter clarifying what submission is and is not. If you're still with me, the next question is, how do I submit to my husband the way God intended?

Submission Plays to Your Strengths

The first thing to understand is that submission is an attitude and not the tasks that you are assigned. Meaning that submission plays to your strengths.

Each individual has her own strengths and weaknesses, submission shines a spotlight on your strengths. In order to be a helpmate, you have to be empowered to handle what your partner is weaker at.

If your husband is terrible with handling the administrative tasks of finances and you're quite good with organizing budgets and numbers, then your version of helping is to handle finances. That still doesn't mean that you put yourself in the leadership role and you make all the final money decisions. What it means, is that you handle the logistics and are the family's financial advisor. If there is a discrepancy or an issue that emerges about money, it's your job to advise and your husband still takes on the burden of the final decision. If he is aware that your advice is gold, the smart move would be for him to do what you suggest - but you should still always allow him the opportunity to lead, even if he's wrong.

Likewise, tasks don't always have to be traditional. For instance, for the first ten years of our marriage, Robert handled much of the cooking. I couldn't cook. Even to this day, my favorite food is ramen noodles and it probably began because it was the only thing I knew how to cook (yes, I am aware of how unhealthy that is).

I remember one instance early in our marriage when I attempted to actually use the kitchen to prepare dinner for Robert and me. I had gotten a Digornio pizza and was very careful to follow each instruction exactly so I wouldn't mess dinner up this time. Step 1: Remove the pizza from the cardboard box. Check. Good so far. Step 2: Remove the plastic wrapping from around the pizza. Done. I was doing really good! Step 3: Place pizza directly on the oven rack. I did just that. I had preheated the oven earlier, so I set the timer and gave myself a pat on the back for a job well done. A few minutes later the smoke detectors went off and I ran into the kitchen to find flames in the oven. I could not, for the life of me, figure out what I did wrong. I followed the instructions exactly! After Robert had put out the fire, he looked in the oven and pulled out a pizza that was still on top of the [burnt] cardboard plate it was packaged on. The directions did not tell me to remove the pizza from the cardboard plate and before putting it into the oven. The direction explicitly stated to put the pizza directly onto the oven rack. It wasn't until Robert explained to me that "directly" was referring to there not being anything in between the pizza and the rack that I finally realized what I did wrong. I took "directly" to mean "put the pizza directly on the oven rack, do not pass go, do not collect $200 and do not remove the cardboard plate."

Needless to say, we didn't have pizza that night and Robert handled most of the cooking - which most would say was very "unwifely" of me. But if my job is to help my husband, the best way I could help was to keep him alive by not attempting to cook.

Whether you clean or your husband cleans or you work outside the home and your husband is a stay-at-home dad or whether you're the one who kills the bugs and your husband is the one consoling the baby to sleep – none of these things are vital to being submissive. It's not so much about what task you are completing as much as it is about your attitude of respecting your husband's authority as the head of the household.

It just so happens that the majority of women and men have a stereotypical set of skills that makes them better in the traditional roles of working husband and stay-at-home mom. However, this does not mean that it applies to everyone. Being a good helpmate means being able to contribute to the marriage the skills that you are great at.

Your Attitude in Submission

I love efficiency. I hate the idea of wasted time – it drives me absolutely crazy. So, if I have 10 things that I need to get done around the house before nightfall and Robert only has 2 things he needs to do, then it seems perfectly efficient for me to ask him to do a couple things from my list so that we can finish at about the same time and relax at the end of the night. Robert strongly disagrees with this mentality, but because he loves me, he helps me out. The problem is, usually by the time he's accomplished a task, he has worn me out emotionally from all the complaining that I think I would've rather just did all 10 tasks myself. Thankfully, he's grown out of that (for the most part).

Nobody likes for someone to help them and complain about it the whole time. The same applies to our submission. We could be technically submitting to our husbands by not fighting for the final decision, but if are grumbling and complaining and "I told you so'ing" the entire time, we're missing the Spirit behind the command.

Submission is about your attitude, not just your actions. Remember, you are not a hired servant. A hired servant can do the job and inwardly complain about it the entire time. A submissive wife submits with joy. She takes pride in being able to support her husband and genuinely respects (or diligently works towards inwardly respecting) him as the head of the household. You cannot submit with joy and be bitter about submitting at the same time.

You have to choose which side you are on or you'll end up making yourself and your husband miserable and you'll miss out on all the advantages of submitting with a joyful heart. There's not much that is more tiring to a man than a wife that is constantly nagging and nitpicking and trying to start a fight. We (trust me, me included) need to learn how to submit with a quiet and gentle spirit. We should exemplify patience with our husbands as they grow into the leaders they are called to be. It's not an overnight process and they certainly cannot do it on their own.

Nia Vardalos is credited for saying that the "man is the head but the woman is the neck, and she can turn the head whichever way she pleases." I really like this analogy. If we take it further we can also note that God created the head to hold the brain and it's the brain that sends the signal to the neck to turn a specific direction. It's also the neck that supports the head and places it at the top of the body. The head and the neck need one another to fulfill what they were created to do. They must work together and be submitted to each other to function correctly. If they are constantly in conflict, then they both receive mixed signals and it causes unneeded strain on the relationship.

Our culture has taught women that strength is personified in the strongest and boldest females out there. But what if strength is really personified in the females that are the most gentle and quiet in spirit?

There is an old Aesop's fable titled "The Wind and the Sun" and it goes something like this: A man is walking across a pasture one day with a cloak wrapped around his neck. The wind and the sun see him and decide to have themselves a friendly competition of strength. Whichever one can separate the cloak from the man fastest will be determined to be the strongest force. The wind goes first. He blows loud and strong – ripping through the trees and high grass. The man's cloak flies behind him, but instead of being ripped away from the man, the man yanks the cloak back to his body and desperately clings it around his body. Despite all its demonstration of strength and boldness, the wind is unsuccessful. It was the sun's turn. He beams brightly, warming up the air and turning up the heat. Within minutes, the man willingly relinquishes his cloak to get relief from the sun's warmth. The sun's warmth proves stronger and mightier than the wind's apparent strength.[5]

Although it doesn't always make sense to us and it certainly may not feel natural, our husbands' hearts are more easily melted than forced open against their wills. When you nag, push, and force, you do nothing more than cause your husband to hold onto his point of view stronger and longer – even if he is wrong and he knows it, the incessant nagging causes him to save face and hold on to his pride.

> *"When they hurled their insults at Him, He did not retaliate; when He suffered, He made not threats. Instead, He entrusted Himself to Him who judges justly... Wives, in the same way submit yourselves to your own husbands so that, if any of them do not believe the Word, they may be won over without words but by the behavior of their wives, when they see the purity and reverence of your lives."*
> *–1 Peter 2:23... 1 Peter 3:1-2 (NIV)*

Even when your husband is nowhere near where he should be, the greatest weapon you have is your submission motivated by your love. Love for God and love for your husband. Your strength is your gentle and quiet spirit. It may take time, but with prayer and your obedience, you'll "help" your husband arrive at where he needs to be and you'll be the one that redeems your marriage.

Submit in Everything

I'm sure we've all heard of people taking scripture out of context. If you've been in a Bible-believing church for any length of time, the preacher has probably made the statement that you can't choose to believe in one verse and not another. The Bible comes as a unit. If you believe it to be true, then all of it is true. It's when we start picking and choosing and taking scripture out of context that we start getting confused. You have to take all scripture and put it together to really get the Spirit of what is being said.

The same is true for submission. If you are going to be submissive in one area, you cannot then choose to be unsubmissive in another area. If you are going to be submissive when he is making the right decisions, then you cannot choose to be unsubmissive when he is making wrong decisions. In fact, it's really only submission when he's making a choice you disagree with and you submit anyway. If you are going to be submissive when he is being an amazing servant-leader, then you cannot choose to be unsubmissive when he is being more of a dictator.

Submission is all encompassing. You do not get to pick and choose the areas of your life you are willing to submit to God and your husband. It's through your complete obedience – and your complete obedience with a joyful heart – that you can start receiving all the blessings that God has for you and your marriage.

At the end of the day, submission is not something I can convince you of. It certainly wasn't something that anyone could convince me of when I first got married. It's something that God may have to reveal to you as you grow in Him. As with many of the concepts in this book, much of it will come naturally as you grow closer to God and allow Him to transform you to be more like Him. My only prayer is that, if nothing else, I have been able to provide some insight that will come back to your memory when the time comes that God does reveal the power behind submission.

It's not a popular word in our culture: Submission. Strongly controversial. Severely misinterpreted. Massively abused. Heavily fought. But if we will put our weapons down and be willing to give God's way a fighting chance, we may just discover how beautiful and powerful being submissive really is.

HOW TO BE MARRIED TO A SUBMISSIVE WIFE

Much of these points were covered in Chapter 3 in greater detail, but if you are a husband reading this and you say to yourself, "there is no way my wife is going to agree with any of this," then there are some things that you can do to start the process to help your wife willingly submit to you:

First, let God lead you. If your wife trusts that God is leading you, she'll be more willing to let you lead her. This means genuinely seeking after Him. Praying and picking up the Bible. Allowing God to transform you into the leader He has called you to be.

Secondly, cherish your wife. Do things that make her feel valuable to you and don't do anything that demeans her.

Third, take responsibility. Be proactive about decisions that need to be made and be willing to admit mistakes. If a decision needs to be made, be the first one to bring it up – or at least don't avoid the conversation.

Fourth, put her needs above your own. Even if it means sacrificing what you want for the well-being of your family. Let your wife see that you are willing to make the hard choices for their betterment.

Last, recognize your need for your wife. Recognize your weaknesses and know that God has provided a helpmate. Empower her to operate in her strengths and let her know how much you need her support.

OUR PERCEPTION OF DECEPTION

#honesty

culture • A lie is sometimes necessary to keep the marriage happy
counter-culture • The truth is always necessary to make the marriage better

five

OUR PERCEPTION OF DECEPTION

We are all familiar with the saying "honesty is the best policy" – yet our culture behaves as if this is seriously outdated information…so much so, that many people don't even realize that they're being dishonest. Before you tell yourself "I don't lie to my spouse" and move on to the next chapter, you should know that honesty isn't just about lying verbally. Having honesty within our marriages means building a foundation of trust in all areas.

WHY WE DECEIVE

Several years ago, I (Gloria) was having a conversation with an unmarried friend of mine over our perceptions of marriage. She didn't seem to care about ever getting married and my knee-jerk response was "don't you want to have a relationship with someone who knows your every thought, deepest secrets and darkest struggles and is there to support you and help you work through all those insecurities so you can approach life with more confidence?" Judging by the disgust and shock on her face, I realized that that probably wasn't the best-selling point for marriage. She didn't want any other human being to be able to access the deep recesses of her mind or heart. She seemed perfectly content with handling the inner hardships of life solo. As I contemplate that conversation, I can't help but try to understand if some people just prefer to keep secrets between them and God or if there is a deeper reason why an individual would prefer to avoid opening up to someone else.

But marriage comes down to an issue of trust. For men, they need to be able to trust that if they let down their walls they'll still be respected. And women need to trust that if they open up their hearts, the contents will be handled with care and love – not judgement. If we don't trust our spouse, then we tend to keep things hidden and attempt to handle things on our own.

Most people trust themselves. Some people trust God and will confess things to him, but we have found that a vast majority of people don't trust their spouses. Yes, they committed their lives to them and love them, but trust them with the inner recesses of their minds and hearts? That's an entirely different story.

However, God created marriage to be a union where a man and a woman can be free to be themselves – no facades, no secrets, no hidden agendas. Without a firm foundation of trust in your marriage, marriage ends up feeling like a windowless jail cell with no escape instead of feeling like a safe haven where you can breathe easy with freedom in your heart and mind. Every individual needs someone they can confidently confide in. There can be mentors and advisors, but that primary confidante should be your spouse.

THE WAYS WE DECEIVE

So what keeps people from being completely honest in their marriages? It boils down to two reasons: selfishness to get what they want and/or fear that their opinions and desires will not be well received. We have broken down deception into four different categories, the first of which is the most obvious.

Deception #1: Lying

When we present the topic of honesty in marriage, the first thing most people think of is lying – telling your spouse something that you know is not true. We don't really need to go into further explanation on this type of deception. It's wrong, you shouldn't do it.

But what about those innocent, polite, little white lies? Are those wrong too? Somehow, we've become a culture that readily accepts the necessity of white lies to "keep the peace." At some point in history, people joked that if a woman asks if she looks fat in her jeans, a man's response should always be "no baby, you look fantastic" - even if the exact opposite is actually true. Whether that advice was initially said as a joke or as serious advice, what has happened culturally is that it has become an accepted truth on how to make your marriage work. And yet, it couldn't be further from the truth.

Marriages do not withstand the test of time by filling the cracks with little white lies. With that said, there are definitely appropriate and inappropriate ways to be honest within your marriage – not everything has to be said bluntly and rudely to be considered "honest," but it definitely should be honest. Even in those seemingly insignificant white lies, there are negative seeds that are planted that can eventually overgrow your marriage.

Deception #2: Withholding

This second deception is also obvious to the moral individual but considered a gray area for the less convicted. Withholding is allowing your spouse to believe something inaccurate by withholding information.

This can range from something that you didn't tell your spouse because "they didn't ask" (even though you know they're approach to the situation would be different if they had all the details), keeping secret accounts or not allowing them to have access to your phone or something as innocent as telling your spouse that something is "ok" when the reality is, it's not "ok."

This is especially true for the females in the world (although some males do it too). The world has just accepted that females don't say what they mean. If a husband asks if his wife minds if he goes out to play golf and she responds with "yea, that's fine." Then, it should be fine. If you are not okay with your spouse doing something, then say it. If you feel a certain way, your reaction shouldn't be to lie and pretend you are okay with something and then yell at your spouse when they took you at your word. You cannot expect an individual to make an informed decision if they do not have all the information.

The deception of withholding goes beyond not communicating tangible information. Allowing your spouse to believe a false reality because they do not know what's in your heart is also a form of deception. For example, allowing your spouse to believe that you are fully committed to them when in fact you have developed an attraction for someone else is a form of withholding. That may sound deep, but it happens far more often than anyone cares to admit.

Everything in marriage is shared - bringing us back to the "one flesh" concept. There is absolutely nothing in your life that your spouse should not have access to. There is no such thing as privacy within marriage. Having an open line of communication between your heart and your spouse's heart is a method of safeguarding your marriage. It should never be a question of whether or not you share something with your spouse, it should only be a matter of when and how.

Deception #3: Flattery

Flattery is also a form of deception. It may not be outright lying, but it's still telling your spouse something that may (or may not) be true but with ulterior motives.

Deception is a heart issue. You may be communicating truth or behaving honestly, but if you are doing so for a different reason than your spouse believes, then it's still deception. What motivates your actions matters to God and to your spouse.

Romans 16:18 makes reference to people who are not trying to serve Christ but only trying to serve themselves. In this verse, these individuals are described as people who "talk smoothly and through flattery they deceive the hearts of the naïve."

Flattery may seem innocent and fun at first – when a husband tells his wife "how pretty you look" when he's in the mood for sex or when a wife tells her husband what a "big, strong man you are" when she wants something on the honey-do list done asap. These statements may in fact be true, but it's flattery when you are saying them for selfish reasons.

We're all probably guilty of such flattery. When we flatter each other, it may be in good fun and the flattery and real intent is obvious, but we must still be careful with this type of deception. The last thing you want is for there to be so much "fun" flattery within your marriage that a lack of trust begins to develop and grow. If you give your spouse a genuine compliment with no strings attached and their immediate response is "what do you want?" you may want to consider if your flattery has started to cause a breakdown of honesty within your marriage.

Deception #4: Manipulation

Manipulation has gotten a bad rap the last couple decades. The ability to manipulate something – exercising your influence to get the results that you desire – is not always a negative or bad thing at its core meaning but again, motivation matters. Manipulation has now turned into a word that carries a connotation of deception, so that's the concept of manipulation that we are going to run with in this book.

There are three ways that manipulation in marriage can be deceptive: withholding information, bribes and threats.

We've already discussed withholding but want to reiterate it under this section. Let's say the wife wants to go on a beach trip with her friends and needs to discuss it with her husband. She intentionally chooses to discuss it with him while he's watching the game because she knows he won't be paying complete attention. Then when she pitches it to him, she tells him all about how hard she works and how much she needs a break, but she doesn't tell him that it's going to cost $800 that they don't have and that he'll have to give up his entire weekend watching the kids on his own. He's not thinking it through clearly because he's preoccupied and says he thinks it's a great idea. If you can picture this scenario, then you can also predict that this is probably going to turn into an argument later. This is manipulation of data. No, there was no lying involved or flattery, but information that would cause her husband to be unsupportive of the decision was intentionally withheld so that the wife could get her way.

Secondly, spouses manipulate each other with bribery – doing things and expecting things in return. For example, a husband who does the dishes for the sole purpose of having sex with his wife that night or a wife that has sex with her husband in exchange for control in their relationship. We're not saying you can never exchange responsibilities or negotiate how responsibilities are divvied up, but when you start bartering and bribing with things that rightfully belong to your spouse or you should be doing out of love in the first place, then this turns into a form of manipulation.

The last form of manipulation is closely related to the second – threats. This is the worst kind of manipulation. A financial provider who threatens to walk out on the family or a spouse that threatens to withhold sex out of anger or until they get what they want is someone who is using manipulation to force their spouse's hand.

For there to be honesty and trust in your relationship, your spouse has to be able to trust that you are committed to the marriage and nothing that was promised at the marriage altar is subject to removal for any reason.

DECEPTION HURTS

So what happens when deception finds its way into your marriage? The first thing it does is breach our marital security. Our spouses should never have to decide whether or not we're being completely honest. Each spouse should be able to trust their spouses, their actions and what they say, so much so, that further proof of their honesty is not required.

For instance, if your spouse tells you they are sorry, it should only be said if they are really sorry. If they are really sorry, and there is a foundation of honesty and trust in the marriage, then you should believe that they are truly sorry and they shouldn't need to provide any proof beyond that (flowers, groveling, a period of cold shouldering, etc.).

If there has been a breach in marital security already, then it may take a while to rebuild trust and proof of your statements may be necessary, but being able to take what your spouse says at face value is the place that we ultimately want to get to within our marriages. You should desire to become trustworthy, to be the person that your husband or wife can trust and feel secure with physically, emotionally and spiritually.

WHITE LIES MATTER
It's easy for us to think of honesty in terms of the big forms of deception: cheating, money, etc. But let's not forget that breaches in our marital security can start at the smallest level of deception.

Let's go back to the jeans example as it's the most culturally popular justification for allowing dishonesty in your marriage.

Your wife walks in the room and asks "do these jeans make me look fat?" Culture has taught us that every husband's answer should be nothing short of "you look amazing." However, let's say she doesn't actually "look amazing". Let's say, the truth is, the jeans are WAY too tight and even though her husband loves her curves, the jeans are not flattering for her full figure nor are they appropriate for the public. I'm sure you've seen such a display of unflattering wardrobe somewhere, so I'll spare you the detailed description. Nevertheless, she trusts her husband, feels confident and happily bounces (pun intended) out the door.

She spends all day at work (it's casual Friday) and then meets her girlfriend for their weekly coffee chat before heading home. When she walks in the coffee shop doors, her girlfriend is shocked, as evident by the look of sheer disgust on her face. The wife is clueless. The first thing out of her girlfriend's mouth is "What. Are. You. Wearing? Those jeans are not doing it for you. At. All." If your friends aren't as blunt, replace the above comment with something more polite. However it's communicated by her girlfriend, the point is, the truth comes out.

The wife's reaction? Her first thought is probably "I knew I shouldn't have trusted my husband." She may not know how to express it, but she immediately feels betrayed, lied to and vulnerable. The one human being in her life that was supposed to be the largest provider of security for her, just publicly ripped that security out from under her and humiliated her in the process. Her husband lied to her. He gave her the false confidence to walk around all day, around all her co-workers, client and friends in clothes that she would normally be utterly embarrassed about. From that moment on, the wife decides that she can't trust her husband's opinion, but she's thankful she can always trust her best girlfriend.

This may seem like a trivial example with an extreme response but what if you replaced one instance with dozens. What if this happened regularly in your marriage as it does with so many. Eventually that response does occur. And from there arises a culture that values the relationship between a wife and her best girlfriends or a husband and his boys over the relationship within a marriage and that's where the breach begins.

There's absolutely nothing wrong with having great friends and mentors. In fact, it's something everyone should have. But when you have a greater sense of security with your friends than you do with your spouse, it may be time to evaluate if and how deception has made its way into your marriage.

MOVING TOWARDS HONESTY

Whether you are rebuilding or maintaining the trust in your marriage, any form of deception hinders honesty. Every statement you make to your spouse, no matter how insignificant, is a decision to build towards an honest marriage or a dishonest marriage. There is no middle ground.

Honesty has to start somewhere. Like many things in marriage, it's a cycle. You may not feel like those little forms of deception have breached the security and trust between you and your spouse, but is it helping honesty to grow in your marriage? If you're not cultivating honesty in your marriage, then chances are, you're diminishing.

Deception puts a crack in the foundation of your marriage. While deception may appear to provide a temporary fix, you damage your marriage in the long-run.

Everything that is hidden, comes out eventually – and it is best if the truth comes from you. If the truth is revealed by any other means, it could permanently destroy your marriage. By keeping a secret or deceiving your spouse on any level, you are only setting yourself up for failure eventually.

Be Honest with Yourself
In order to be honest with your spouse, you have to be honest with yourself and God. Analyze your motivations and intentions carefully and prayerfully. Make sure that you aren't trying to justify your deceptive actions. No matter what your justifications are, deception is deception. Two wrongs don't make a right.

Be an Open Book
The only thing wrongs do, are add up to more wrongs. But rights have the ability to subtract wrongs. Even if your spouse behaves a certain way or doesn't understand you or a situation, countering with deception only makes things worse.

The quickest route between two points is a straight line; every unknown piece of information is a loophole and every flatter and manipulation is a detour. If you want to get to that place of "oneness" that God intends for marriages, then you have to be willing to be an open book. You cannot be "one" if there are parts of you that your spouse doesn't know about.

There should be no secrets. No unknown passwords or hidden accounts. No past tragedies, no situations that you haven't told your spouse about yet. No unresolved feelings or situations. Nothing that you keep from your spouse because you think you can handle it on your own or because you think your spouse can't handle it.

Sin is created in the darkness. Anything you keep hidden in the dark, only feeds on itself and grows. If you want to bring resolution to something in your life or in your marriage, you have to bring it into the light. It's only in the light that God can take over and bring healing to past hurts, hidden feelings, deeply rooted trust issues or struggles and strongholds that you've dealt with all your life.

> *"For there is nothing covered that will not be revealed,*
> *nothing hidden that will not be known."*
> *—Luke 12:2*

Honesty Doesn't Deserve Punishment

As you make steps to mend or grow the security in your marriage through honesty, remember to communicate with love and grace. How you give and receive truth either reinforces or punishes your spouse for their decision to be honest with you.

Just because something is true, doesn't mean it has to be said harshly. You can be honest and loving at the same time. If your wife comes in the room and asks "do these jeans make me look fat?" Replying with "Baby, I always think you look beautiful and I love your curves but those jeans are not highlighting your best features as well as other jeans would" is just as honest as "Woah! You look like a cow!"

We're ragging on the husbands a lot with this jeans illustration, but the same is especially true the other way around. Wives can be the worst when it comes to brutal honesty. Husbands need encouragement and they need to know that their wives support them. Padding a negative truth with multiple positive truths (not positive lies) communicates what needs to be communicated while still encouraging your spouse.

Wives, if you truly desire an open and honest marriage where you feel safe, secure and able to take your husbands' words at face value, then you have to be willing to receive that open and honest communication without throwing a temper tantrum and starting a fight every time you hear something that you do not like. Let that marinate for a minute.

Communication is a two-way street. Think about your cell phone. It is a communications device. It does two things, it sends AND receives information. If it didn't do both of those jobs well, you would replace it. The same is true in our marriages, we have to be able to send information with love but we must RECEIVE information with love as well. If your spouse believes you're going to blow up if they share their heart, or tell you about a problem, or ask for help, they'll eventually just withhold information. You have to be able to receive information with love, even if it's painful, in order to maintain openness and honesty.

If you want to be able to trust your spouse, then your spouse has to be able to trust that their truth is safe (physically and emotionally) with you.

Back to the jeans illustration. There is a reason that culture tells the husband to lie to their wives regarding whether or not the jeans make her look fat. Culture teaches him that if he tells her the truth, he's going to get blasted for it. So the answer is simple. Don't blast your spouse for telling you the truth.

How you give and receive truth either reinforces or punishes your spouse for their decision to be honest with you.

Grow Up
Learn some selflessness. Be careful not to use your power within the marriage to get what only you want and what only you want now.

If you feel like you want something that requires you to deceive or bribe your spouse in order to get it, you should evaluate if what you're asking for is selfish and who it will ultimately benefit or hurt in the end.

Being deceptive has its roots in selfishness but being defensive can be just as selfish. Proverbs 18:2 says "a fool has no delight in understanding, but in expressing his own heart." Defensiveness communicates that you are only interested in yourself. Instead of reacting out of your immediate emotions, take the time to understand what is being said and why it's being said. Your spouse's perception might be wrong, but you can't truly adjust their perception of something until you can correct it from their viewpoint.

Have patience with your spouse. It's not your responsibility to point out every flaw in them or change them. It's your job to be the husband or wife that God has called you to be and, in the process, pray for your spouse continually and God will change their heart. You will only push your spouse away if you try to change them by taking the reins from God and aborting what He has called you to be as a husband or wife.

A Relationship of Accountability

Form a relationship of accountability with your spouse. It's awesome to have other accountability partners and mentors in your life – it's scriptural. But we strongly believe that your primary "accountability partner" should be your spouse. If your marriage isn't quite there yet, then of course lean on your mentor to help you get there – but don't let your mentor replace your spouse in the area of accountability in your life. You should be working towards a relationship with your spouse where both of you can help each other grow closer to God.

Accountability doesn't mean that your spouse is your probation officer. They aren't there for you to have to report to or to punish you every time you slip and fall. Your spouse is your partner, your helpmate. Accountability partners are equals – one isn't more superior than the other. You are both there to lovingly guide each other through life. But in order to have that type of relationship, both spouses need to be willing to be open, loving and submitted to each other.

This concept of being your spouse's accountability partner doesn't give either spouse permission to start pointing out every flaw they see in their spouse. But it does mean, that you should give your spouse permission to point something out if there is an area of your life that you may be blinded to – and when they do – it's your job not to get angry and defensive. Remember, that your spouse is not against you, they are for you.

> *"Faithful are the wounds of a friend,*
> *but the kisses of an enemy are deceitful."*
> *–Proverbs 27:6*

Use Wisdom

We strongly urge you to use wisdom in applying what you've read in this chapter about honesty.

Being honest doesn't mean that you should go home and air out all your dirty laundry all at once. Every marriage is in a different place and season and every situation will need to be handled differently. If you happen to be someone that has a lot of serious dirty laundry to air out, the best advice we can give you is to get counseling for how to best handle your specific situation.

Working your way toward an honest and open relationship doesn't mean that you now have to start voicing your opinion on everything your spouse does or confessing every fleeting, unclean thought you have. The last thing you want to do is create an atmosphere in your marriage that is open and honest but also negative and hurtful. There is a balance between being totally honest and brutally negative. Ask God for the wisdom to know where that balance is.

START NOW, START SMALL

Practicing an open and honest relationship can seem like such a trivial matter that we can tend to overlook the little seeds of deception we innocently plant in our marriage over time. The greatest benefits of establishing honesty in the routine events of your marriage now may not become truly evident until you are faced with a major ordeal.

We've faced a couple of these difficult seasons in our relationship and we strongly believe that it was because of the pre-established culture of honesty in our marriage that we were able to notice the smallest of deceptions early on and help each other on the road to recovery with love and grace, despite the immense pain and hurt that we both felt.

If we would've waited until something catastrophic happened before we started establishing these foundational principals in our marriage, it may have been too late. It may have been too much to deal with the crisis-at-hand and years of bad habits from a marriage built on a shaky foundation. Ultimately, we may not have made it through with our marriage still intact.

What the enemy meant to destroy us is now something that can be used as a testimony to what a marriage can look like when flawed humans operate on God's terms.

There are numerous times that we don't feel like God's rules necessarily apply to us because we don't see the immediate negative repercussions of running our marriage culturally instead of Biblically. But God knows and sees all things.

Deception is one of the enemy's greatest tools against a marriage. Eliminating all forms of deception now, no matter how small and trivial, will allow you to begin to fully experience the security, openness and "oneness" that God intended for your marriage. A marriage that can withstand whatever waves come your way.

FIGHTING FAIRLY

#arguing

culture • Avoiding conflict keeps the marriage together
counter-culture • Learning how to work through conflict makes a marriage successful

six

FIGHTING FAIRLY

Have you ever met a couple that says "oh, we never fight?" We have. A few things come to mind when we hear that: either they are so mature in their marriage that any disagreements are calmly dealt with in a nice conversation over dinner, or their definition of "fighting" is different than ours or they have a slew of unresolved issues and both parties are trying to keep the peace by not saying anything and eventually they are going to explode.

The first possibility sounds unrealistic, but we think it's a very real goal that can be achieved the more spiritually mature we become (i.e. physical maturity does not equal spiritual maturity). The second issue with the differing definition of "fight" is something we'll address before we start this chapter so we're all starting on the same page.

The third possibility is where I think many couples fall prey to – they just avoid fighting by not bringing up the issues. That doesn't mean they don't have issues, it just means they are going unresolved. But in order to have a healthy marriage, we have to learn to have a constantly open dialogue between ourselves and our spouses – even if that means working through the occasional disagreement.

ARGUING IS NOT A BAD THING

The more we communicate, the more we get to know each other. The caveat here is that the more we get to know each other, the more differing opinions we'll come across. So it seems that our only happy options in marriage are to either not communicate at all or communicate and "fight" all the time. But there is a third option – communicate and learn to "fight fairly" or in less-catchy terms, learn how to disagree without fighting.

All these words – disagree, argue, fight – are so often used interchangeably, but they have very different definitions. According to Merriam-Webster: To disagree is to simply "have a different opinion or to fail to agree." To argue is to "cause (someone) to decide to not do something by giving reasons." Now, to "fight" is to be "involved (in a battle, struggle, etc.) or to argue in an angry way." What we really want to avoid in our marriages, is the fighting. However, the disagreeing and arguing is an essential part of healthy communication in our marriage.

It's so sad for us to see how many people view arguing as a negative trait in marriages (arguing by the actual definition of arguing). Disagreeing with your spouse's opinion on how to handle a situation and then giving them reasons to try to convince them to agree with you, is not negative at all! Being able to express your feelings freely with your spouse and work together as a team to resolve issues even when you have opposing opinions, only serves to strengthen your marriage.

Learning to communicate with your spouse is the first step to resolving ANY issue in your marriage – if there is no acknowledgement of a problem, there can be no resolution. Things and situations that are painful will occur in our marriage and when they do, we must learn to allow them to draw us together, not apart.

At the end of the day, the issue is not that you disagree with your spouse – God created you to provide a different opinion than your spouse so that you can be a helpmate or leader to them and assist in creating a balanced life. Arguing is beneficial to marriage as it provides a platform to discuss the reasons why you disagree. The issue then, is that we learn HOW to argue so that it doesn't turn into a fight. Leo Tolstoy once said "what counts in making a happy marriage is not so much how compatible you are, but how you deal with incompatibility."

THE THREE CS TO GOOD COMMUNICATION

We've developed what we call the "three C's to good communication." They've become so in-grained in our marriage that we now use them as verbal darts to throw at each other when we get into a knock-down, drag-out fight (that's a joke, sort of). But in all seriousness, prior to developing these "3 C's", we really did have fights that people would've paid to see. Once we were able to write-out these three foundational elements of good communication, it completely transformed how we argue. It's only when we break one of these rules, that things turn into a fight.

What we believe to be the three key essentials to good communication are the ability to: Consent to Communicate, Communicate Calmly and Communicate Concisely.

CONSENT TO COMMUNICATE

Consent to Communicate is when both spouses agree to be willing to speak about anything in your life truthfully and not withholding anything.

Commit to a Resolution

We live in a "flight" culture. If we encounter resistance or a problem, we just leave. Someone say something at church that we don't like? We just find a new church. Get in a spat with a co-worker or our boss gets on our last nerve? We just find a new job. Friend decides to side with someone else in an argument? Find a new friend. Spouse can't do anything right with no hopes of improving? Find a new spouse.

Leaving the problematic situation is always the easiest way out but it never provides the opportunity for character or spiritual growth. It's the commitment aspect of marriage that forces us to learn to work through our conflict. It's our commitment to marriage that helps us to grow as individuals so that God can more fully use us for the purpose He has called us to. If we never learn to deal with hard situations, then we may never learn character traits such as grace, patience, self-control, humility, gratitude, perseverance, diligence, obedience and the list goes on and on. It's the lack of these traits that may end up keeping you from experiencing the fullness of life that God intends for us to live.

Consenting to communicate means committing to resolving the situation. Resolution doesn't always mean that both spouses will ultimately agree, but it does mean that both spouses are going to resolve that working in unity has a higher importance than being right. Committing to resolve the situation also does not mean that once an argument starts, no one can leave until it's resolved. Sometimes, we need to take some time to calm down before we can think things through with any amount of intelligence and some situations can't be resolved in one conversation. Committing to resolve the situation means that no matter what it takes to get there, at the end of the day, you and your spouse are still committed to each other.

Ignorance is not Bliss

Glossing over problems and not discussing them or bringing them up is NOT working through conflict. It's pretending there isn't a problem and that's the same thing as running from the problem. It is a delayed reaction because eventually, those things will surface in one way or another and most likely they will surface on a far more serious issue.

Ephesians 4:25 states, "...no more lies, no more pretense. Tell your neighbor the truth. In Christ's body, we're all connected to each other, after all. When you lie to others, you end up lying to yourself." In other words, communicate. Remember that you can lie by withholding information. If you don't talk about the problem, then you are giving the pretense to your spouse that there is no problem.

Make sure you use balance and wisdom in your communication. Just because we are encouraging everyone to communicate everything doesn't mean you should start criticizing your spouse. On the other hand, if something really bothers you on a regular basis, don't decide not to communicate it with your spouse because you simply don't want to hurt their feelings.

If something is consistently bothering you, but you never mention that issue out of concern for their feelings, what do you think is happening to you emotionally? You will slowly drift away from your spouse and eventually, bitterness and resentment will surface and you won't know where it came from. If you had addressed the issue earlier, when it was smaller, it may have never reached that point.

Timing is Everything

As we mentioned in the previous chapter, in order for communication to exist, there has to be information given and received. Consenting to communicate means waiting for the right time when information can be received. For instance, a wife walking in the middle of a football game trying to discuss something is usually not going to find a very receptive husband.

For us, when Gloria is working, she's 100% invested in what she's doing. She's not capable of walking and chewing gum at the same time or walking and texting or holding two different conversations or "multi-tasking". She's capable of a lot of things, but what makes her so great at her job is that she's completely focused on the task-at-hand and doesn't get distracted by the chaos around her. I (Robert) love that about her. At the same time, if she's in the middle of writing an email, I know she's going to get pretty frustrated if I want to talk about something unrelated to what she's doing. In fact, it just happened about one-minute ago while writing this. There's nothing like an in-the-moment illustration to support your point.

No, maybe she shouldn't get frustrated. But I also believe that I shouldn't assume that what I need to talk about has to be talked about right at that moment and that it is more important than what she is working on. We have to have grace and understanding in our relationship. You know how your spouse works and the things that they can handle and the timing of when they can handle it. It's your responsibility as a loving partner to assist them in being an effective communicator in your marriage.

Consenting to Communicate with Each Other

Consenting to communicate means that we consent to communicate with our spouses – not to our best friend, our parents or our social media followers.

Social media ranting has become rampant in today's marriages. There's no faster way to get the verbal support and backup from dozens of "friends" than by posting your spouse's ridiculousness on social media. People love drama and they love voicing their opinions – even if it's none of their business. It's a rare situation that a mature friend is going to reply to your post and tell you how wrong you actually are. Most all of your status responses will be in support of your side. This does two things: one, gives you emotional ammo to stick to your guns and not require yourself to grow spiritually in anyway; and two, slanders your spouse in a very public forum – causing them embarrassment, feelings of betrayal and a refusal to repent, even if what they did was legitimately wrong. So even if what your spouse did was absolutely disgraceful, most of the time you've done far more damage by posting about it and it's a longer road to recovery.

Additionally, going to your friends or parents ranting about your spouse's argument can be just as damaging – especially when venting to your family. Consider this. You get into a fight with your spouse and run to your brother's house where your parents are also visiting. You tell them all about your horrible spouse. They comfort you, support you and get angry at your spouse with you. You finally decide to go back home and after a long night, you resolve things with your spouse and all is forgiven. However, your brother and your parents didn't get to experience the same resolution that you experienced. They're still angry and even though you say everything is fine now, they still have remnants of emotions of disdain toward your spouse.

It's true, when you get married, you leave your mother and father and cleave to your spouse. However, you are all still connected as family and now you have to deal with the drama of your family not liking your spouse. You cause drama every time you run to family when you and your spouse get in a fight. Do you run to them with the same zeal when there's something about your spouse to brag about?

We aren't saying not to get counsel. Counsel is extraordinarily important. Proverbs 11:14 tells us that "in the multitude of counselors there is safety" (NKJV). But make sure that you are exercising discernment in who you get counsel from and that you are actually getting counsel and not just venting to someone when you should be communicating with your spouse.

COMMUNICATE CALMLY

The second "C" is learning to communicate calmly. That means being calm when bringing up an issue and not responding or speaking harshly or rashly in a response to that issue. I think everyone reading this can attest to the fact that responding or speaking harshly in an argument almost immediately escalates the argument to a fight.

> *"...let every man be swift to hear, slow to speak, slow to wrath; for the wrath of man does not produce the righteousness of God."*
> *—James 1:19-20 (NKJV)*

How to Hear It

If you get upset every time your spouse tells you something that you don't like, then it will be nearly impossible for them to be honest with you and work through things together. We've already touched on honesty in a relationship, this is the other half of it. If you want an open, honest relationship, then you have to learn to receive that communication calmly or else you squander any attempts your spouse may have had in consenting to communicate.

I (Gloria) remember one particular time when Robert and I were sitting in the same business meeting. I felt like the meeting was going well. I was getting a lot of my opinions across and it seemed to be well-received. We all took a quick break and it was during this break that Robert pulled me aside and with a firm tone said "Gloria, you are talking WAY too much and you're hijacking the meeting." It's at this point that I had two options: get offended that he would dare point out a well-known flaw of mine or be grateful that we have a relationship where he feels he can keep me safe. My immediate emotional response was the former, but it only took me a couple seconds to realize that the way I really felt was the latter. I didn't want to be known as the person who talked so much that I didn't care what everyone else thought or as someone who had such an inflated sense of self-importance that only what I said mattered. I wanted to be known as someone who could collaborate, a team player, a professional. Bottom line: I wasn't (and am still not) perfect, so if there was anyone that should have permission to protect me from myself, it should be my spouse. Robert was protecting me and my reputation and I appreciated that we had a relationship where he could do that without it causing a fight later.

Perception is reality. You may not feel that what your spouse is saying has any bearing on what is actually happening. However, if that is the way that they are perceiving what is happening, then to them, that perception is their reality. Listen to them and truly try to understand your spouse. Even if you think what they are saying is ridiculous, they wouldn't say it if it wasn't true to them.

How to Say It

"But, speaking the truth in love, may grow up in all things into Him who is the head – Christ."
–Ephesians 4:15 (NKJV)

In the same way that you should receive honest communication without getting upset, it's equally important that when you give honest communication that you are doing so out of love. We're not saying that the only time you say something to your spouse is when it is exclusively for their benefit and when you feel like you love them. We're saying that you should be cautious with your words when you are angry and feeling hateful or bitter about something.

How news is delivered is just as important as the news itself. If you are angry about something, that is not the time to burst in the room and start yelling at your spouse. Remember, communicate calmly. If you genuinely want to discuss something, yelling is not going to get your message across as effectively as discussing it. It may give you temporary results but learning to talk things through calmly will give you far more permanent results and establish a culture of respect in your marriage.

When to Say It

It's not always just a matter of responding to your spouse calmly. You can say the right thing the right way and it still escalate the argument because it was said in the wrong order.

Even in our Christian walk, there is a clear order that God takes us through to mature us spiritually. As outlined in Chad Craig's book, "Divine Design for Discipleship", the foundation of our relationship with God is understanding that we are fully accepted by Him regardless of our past, present or future failures. It's only after our foundation is firm that God can effectively begin to "fix" our behavior. Christians who focus on fixing their behavior before having the security of God's love for them, tend to end up frustrated, self-hating and judgemental.[1]

The same goes for your relationship with your spouse. If you immediately attempt to fix or correct an issue before you express validation - even if what you are saying is correct - you can end up creating contempt in your marriage. However, if you take the time to reassure your spouse that you understand and love them, then you create a safe environment where you can fix the situation or address your spouse's behavior.

ESEF - Empathize, Support, Encourage, Fix

We developed an acronym to help us remember this concept and it has proven highly effective in our discussions at deterring potential fights. This acronym isn't just effective for marriages but we've also found it useful in our work and family relationships.

E is for empathize. Empathizing with your spouse when they are upset doesn't mean they are correct in how they feel, but it does communicate that they are valued and how they feel matters. It's saying things that validate them, like "that's tough", "I'm sorry you're having a bad day", "that would make me mad too."

S is for support. Supporting your spouse verbally communicates that not only are they valued and their feelings matter, but you are there to help them no matter what the situation. Statements like "is there anything I can do to help?" or giving them a hug communicates that you are available for them.

E is for encourage. Encouraging your spouse gives them hope in the situation so they can focus on how to fix the problem later. Saying "It'll be ok", "God has a plan" or "this season will pass" are all ways to express encouragement.

F is for fix. Finally, after your spouse feels secure in their relationship with you, then you can both work together to fix the issue.

Sleeping Angry

> "Be angry, and do not sin: do not let the sun go
> down on your wrath, nor give place to the devil."
> —Ephesians 4:26 (NKJV)

If you've been in the church world for any amount of time, you are probably already familiar with this verse. When we first got married, Gloria and I took this verse to heart. We interpreted it as meaning that every argument had to be resolved before we went to bed. So we would yell, scream and sometimes cry while fighting until 3am – all the while getting more tired and more delirious. But we kept at it until we were both so exhausted that we just gave up so we could go to sleep. I'm sure many of you can relate. We don't recommend approaching this verse in the same way. What this verse is not saying is that if you go to sleep angry, your marriage is doomed to fail.

However, take note of the last part of this sentence, the portion that often gets left off, "…nor give place to the devil." The ESV translation says, "…and give no opportunity to the devil." So if you read it from a cause-reaction perspective, what the verse is actually stating is that when we let the sun go down on our anger, we are giving opportunity to the devil. Opportunity for what? Opportunity for bitterness, resentment and unforgiveness to settle in our hearts.

When we make it a habit and a marital lifestyle to go to bed angry, we are making it a habit to hold onto our anger instead of releasing it through grace towards our spouse. Learning to release our anger before we call it a day, regardless of the resolution of the argument, gets us into the habit of being quick to forgive. It's a Biblical instruction that ends up protecting us from allowing the enemy to steal our joy and peace, the joy and peace that is rightfully ours through Christ.

In fact, it's backed by science as well. Neuroscientists at UMass Amherst found that if you have a negative emotional response to something – like anger or sadness – the response is reduced if you stay awake afterwards. If you go to sleep immediately, the response becomes "protected". Once a response is "protected", when you are exposed to the effect again – for instance, if it was your spouse who caused that negative response – your negative response will be just as negative as the first time. So in essence, by going to sleep while angry at something your spouse said or did, you are training your brain to respond with the same negative intensity the next time your spouse does or says the same thing. If you learn to let go of your anger before going to sleep, the next time your spouse does or says the same anger-inducing thing, you'll have a better chance of responding with more grace and less anger.

Which brings us to the question: "so if the Stella's advise against arguing until 3am until the situation is resolved and the Bible says to not let the sun go down on your anger, what are they suggesting?" We'd like to point out that the Bible clearly says, "do not let the sun go down on your wrath." It does not say, "do not let the sun go down until the argument is resolved."

The reality is, many of the issues and problems in our marriage won't get a resolution overnight. In fact, there are some issues that both of us may never see eye-to-eye on. On top of that, trying to argue when you are emotional, stressed and overtired is a waste of time and only leads to bigger arguments. So we have to learn to be able to disagree with our spouses. We may not like what they did or said, but we do not need to be angry about it.

This is an ugly world and ugly things happen every minute of every day. We cannot go around being fueled by anger to the point that we are dwelling on how angry we are about something all the time. In life and in marriage, we have to learn to LET THINGS GO. We cannot fix everything in the world and we cannot fix everything about our spouses. Only God can change our spouse. Certainly, we can discuss our concerns with our spouse and help them along their journey, but we are not going to change them. So what's the point in carrying around anger and unforgiveness? The only person unforgiveness harms is us.

At some point, if we are angry about something, we have to immediately counter that anger with grace and forgiveness. Whatever situation occurs, we have to tell ourselves, "No, I don't like what my spouse did. It was an awful, terrible and selfish thing to do. It was not right. And yes, it's very aggravating that they actually think they didn't do anything wrong. And no, I do not feel understood and it's not fair. But Jesus forgave me. I will never truly understand the depth of the sacrifice that He made for me. It wasn't fair for Him to pay the price for my sins. And even though I know what He did for me, I continue to be selfish and I continue to do things that I know are not pleasing to Him. And yet, He continues to love me. He continues to provide for me. He is committed to me. He continues to extend Grace when I don't deserve it, on a daily basis. When I married my spouse, I made the same commitment to them. To love them no matter what, until I am no longer walking this earth. So yes, what my spouse did is hurtful and I'm left without affirmation, but I'm going to let God deal with this. I'm going to ask God to change this issue in my spouse and I'm going to move forward loving them for the things I love about them and extending grace for the things that I don't like about them." We know, easier said than done.

We know how extremely difficult it can be in the height of our emotions to reel that anger back and extend love and grace instead. But this is the Spirit of Christ. As Jentezen Franklin puts it, "it's better to be reconciled than to be right."[2] The argument doesn't have to be resolved. The fault doesn't have to be confessed to. The situation doesn't have to have a final decision made. But we can make the choice to love our spouse in spite of the argument. If nothing else, while you are lying in bed with your back turned away from your spouse in anger, pray for God to help you release that anger, to help you forgive and to give you wisdom on how to handle the situation. This may shock you, but God will show up, almost immediately and cloak you with a peace that melts away your anger. But you have to be willing to allow God to help you. Don't be so stubborn that you refuse God's peace.

Occasionally, we implement the following strategy in our own marriage: when we get into a heated argument before bed, we give ourselves a few minutes to calm down and pray individually, allowing God to change our hearts, then we say something like, "I'm really tired, I can't think, let's talk about this tomorrow, I love you." The "I love you" part is important (and difficult to say after an unresolved argument) to us because it communicates that this (the argument) isn't over, but this (the marriage) isn't over either. It's reaffirming that whatever the situation, whatever the sin, we love each other and even if we don't feel the emotion of love, we understand the commitment of it.

COMMUNICATE CONCISELY

The last "C" in our "3 Cs of Communication" is communicating concisely. That means being able to stay on the topic of an argument or discussion and resolve the issue.

If other topics and issues suddenly make their way into the conversation, if it's really an issue, agree to save it for another day, tackle one topic at a time. This becomes an issue when spouses try to level the playing field, "oh, you think that something is wrong with me, well, let me tell you how you aren't perfect!" Then before you know it, both of you are spewing insults at each other and you don't even know why you started fighting in the first place.

Staying on topic also means that you don't resort to name calling, insulting or bringing up past hurts. You cannot resolve one issue by bringing to the surface all the other issues and trying to hurt your spouse – it just causes more issues. If during an argument, either spouse starts insulting the other or begins going off on rabbit trails from last week, it's time to take a break. There is absolutely no point in continuing an argument when emotions have taken the place of reason.

They say opposites attract - but in many ways, that wasn't the case for me (Gloria) and Robert. We are both strongly opinionated, extremely stubborn, innately blunt, highly emotional (I'm highly emotional in every way and he's highly emotional with frustration when he feels wronged) and to top it off, we both love debating. During our dating years and early in our marriage, I noticed that arguing and debating seemed to be the equivalent to flirting for us. We liked the challenge of a good debate.

The problem with two people getting together that argue for fun, is that when we had an argument about something legitimate, our argument elevated to a new height and things just got out of hand. Our biggest issues in real arguments were getting off topic and the constant interruptions from both sides – so occasionally when we could no longer argue like civilized human beings face-to-face, we went to our separate corners of the house and finished our argument via text.

Routinely arguing or making serious decisions via text is not something we recommend. For a relationship to be healthy, it's important for a couple to learn how to communicate, disagree and practice self-control in-the-moment and in-person – it's a vital life skill both in and outside of marriage.

With that said, we did find that there were some benefits to an alternate method of communication when face-to-face didn't seem to be working in a particular argument. It allowed us the opportunity to write-out all our frustrations before hitting the send button. Having that chance to vent all our feelings in writing prevented us from saying something in-the-moment that we didn't really mean and allowed us the opportunity to reflect on what we were really arguing about in the first place.

It's not a flawless system by any means nor is it for everyone. But for those that are more accustomed to texting than talking, practicing how to reread texts before you send can sometimes serve as a good transitional tool to get you to the place where you are thinking before you speak. Just keep in mind that you can't manage your relationship entirely via text – it's a useful tool on some occasions, not a replacement for face-to-face interaction.

Say what you Mean

I (Gloria) had to improve on being concise in exactly what I wanted from Robert in an argument. It would be great if Robert could just read my mind, but he can't and it's not fair to him to expect him to. Not all women, but many of us, are terrible at not wanting to explain why we are upset or what we really want. We feel a sense of "I don't want to have to tell him, that's the point, he should already know what he did wrong or what I want." Unfortunately, we just have to accept that's just not the way a guy's brain works. When we can get past that fact, things will go so much easier.

One particular instance several years ago when we were setting up for a marriage event, I (Gloria) was beyond stressed out. I was overtired and at a breaking point. Robert and I got into a fight a couple hours prior to the event and it turned into a pay-per-view event. I honestly don't even know what we were fighting about. I just felt so stressed that I wanted to scream and what I was screaming didn't even have to make sense - I just wanted to scream words. I joke that it was that breaking point that made me realize that I truly felt I could relate to what losing your mind would feel like. I'm not crazy (I don't think), but I certainly felt crazy.

I was so overwhelmed and so stressed and all I truly wanted was for Robert to take control of the situation, hold me and tell me it was going to be ok. Essentially, all I wanted was for him to hug me. But for whatever reason, I couldn't get the words out of my mouth. It seems odd, but I felt as if I was trapped in my own body and I couldn't get the words "I need a hug" out of my mouth, so the frustration exploded out with insanity-like behavior. I was ultimately pushing away the very person I wanted to hold and hug me. I felt trapped. Robert was left clueless and shocked.

Finally, after a couple hours, I think he finally figured out how to read between the screams and he took control of my flailing arms and forced a hug and I melted and the argument was over. In this scenario, the fight was more about me being overwhelmed and needing support than it was about anything that was actually coming out of my mouth.

The problem is, if we aren't concise in our communication, how is our spouse supposed to know what it is we really want and how to respond? So now, when a fight is about to breakout, we try to very concisely ask the other, "I don't know how you want me to respond to this, what is it that you want from me?" At which point, the other spouse pushes aside their desire to be understood without words and replies with, "Right now, I need encouragement" or "Right now, I need a solution" or "Right now, I just want you to be on my side" or "Right now, I need you to point out where I went wrong." It seems so simple, and yet, as adults we make things so complicated.

What we really need to do is analyze for ourselves what it is that we want or need from our spouse in that moment and then tell them. Plain and simple. No games. Just straightforward, concise communication.

THE AFTERMATH

Much like a tornado sweeping through an area and wreaking havoc on everything in its path, after the tornado has passed, the citizens of that town don't just stand up and resume their normal lives as if nothing happened. They have to deal with the aftermath. Many couples will have a massive fight and then once the fight has dissipated, whether it was resolved or not, they wake-up and continue on with life as if nothing happened. But if there is a storm in your marriage, we feel it's valuable to spend time dealing with the aftermath so that things are not left behind to fester or repeat themselves.

Always Apologize

Our culture has made it very clear that in order for a husband to win an argument, he needs to apologize. The woman is always right. The husband is always wrong. At some point, we're sure it started off as a joke. But somewhere along the way, the next generation coming up didn't understand the joke, so they took it as fact and so here we are today.

Here's our opinion on the matter. At the end of every argument, we BOTH genuinely apologize for something. Whether you were right or wrong, there is always SOMETHING you can apologize for. A heated argument or a fight doesn't happen with just one party acting inappropriately. You can apologize because you were legitimately wrong or you can apologize because you argued wrong or because you didn't extend enough grace to begin with. No matter the situation, if a fight breaks out, there's something you did wrong in that situation that you can apologize for.

Fight Recap

Much like replays of a good punch in a pay-per-view fight, it's not a bad idea to recap the fight. This technique isn't always necessary but when you're early in your marriage or even if you've been married for 30 years, this is a great way to expose problems in your arguments in order to begin changing the trend.

Once the fight is over and you and your spouse have had time to cool off and completely get over the situation, have a conversation about it. What made the argument escalate to a fight? What can be done to prevent it from becoming a fight next time? Is there a phrase that your spouse says that sets you off? Or is there a way that your spouse would prefer you to respond that would prevent the fight from starting. This isn't a blaming session or a time to say "if you wouldn't have said this, I wouldn't have responded this way". This is a time for you to examine YOURSELF. Let your spouse learn from their mistakes.

The kicker here is to not allow your recap to turn into another fight. The more you talk about how you and your spouse talk, the more you'll get to know each other and be able to work towards a solution together.

Resolutions

There's a wide array of situations and arguments and each one has a different way that it can be resolved. We can't cover every specific situation, but in general, there are some clear-cut solutions that can bring clarity to an argument.

When the argument results from a decision that needs to be made – after all is said and done (i.e. thorough discussion), husbands should make the decision that is best for the well-being of his wife and children and wives should respect their husband's decision and submit to it with a good attitude. (If this statement offends you and you skipped "Chapter 4: Doormats", you might want to go back and read it.) Even if the husband ultimately decides to make a decision completely contrary to the wife's opinion (which, in a balanced marriage will probably be an extremely rare scenario), it will be necessary for the wife to adjust her attitude and opinions to reflect that of her husbands in order for both spouses to move forward in unity. You cannot live in unity and peace as "one flesh" if you move forward completely split in the final decision.

If the argument resulted from a deep-seated issue that cannot be resolved "overnight"; get counseling, discuss it if/when the time is right but don't force it. Not every argument is black and white. Many arguments are bigger than one argument or one counseling session. Whatever you do, having a negative attitude towards the issue or constantly bringing it up in a nagging fashion, won't help. Discuss it if the time is right, but don't force it into an argument every time or your marriage will be identified by that one issue. And most definitely, get professional counseling to help you navigate serious issues.

If the argument is a result of your spouse's human flaw or when our spouse isn't perfect – just as God extended us grace, we must learn to do the same. Just as we could never fulfill the Old Testament law, our spouse is incapable of always meeting our needs or expectations. We have a bad habit of setting an unrealistic bar of expectation for our spouse but keeping that bar at our feet for ourselves. Every human is flawed, so if you are married, then you are married to someone who is failing in some way. You can respond to those failures in a way that causes you to be a bitter and resentful person or you can respond to those failures in a way that draws you closer to your spouse and closer to God. An argument that starts because your spouse isn't perfect, is an argument that should end because of your knowledge of God's grace.

When an argument is a one-sided effort, give them time to ponder what you've said, pray for them and continue to love them. If one spouse pushes away and the other is trying to make it work, take a lesson from the story of the prodigal son (Luke 15:11-32). You cannot force your spouse to change or make them see it your way. The more you push, the more difficult it will be for them to admit their flaws, apologize or repent. The only thing you can do is pray for them and continue to be obedient to God in extending love and grace to them. God will change your spouse's heart through your behavior.

If an argument or situation arises because your spouse confesses something, forgive and assist; in most cases (not all), your spouse is just as trapped by a sin as you are hurt by it. Try not to keep a mental filing cabinet of all the secrets, weakness and confessions your spouse shares with you. If you choose not to forgive and instead, use confessed knowledge as a weapon, communication will cease. When communication ceases, eventually your marriage will grow stale. On the flip-side, try not to play the victim. We know that's really difficult – we know from the giving and receiving end. But whatever the scenario, try to see what your spouse is struggling with and rise up to encourage and help them. Nothing reflects Christ's character more, shows your love and commitment greater or merits repentance from your spouse faster, than when you continually love them after they have betrayed you in some way. We're certainly not saying to ignore the issue or that your spouse is blameless in their confession. We're suggesting that you adjust your battle plans. Instead of fighting your spouse, recognize the sin or bondage they are in and refocus your fight towards that target.

MORE MONEY, MY MONEY, NO MONEY

#finances

culture • Finances in marriage should be handled separately to avoid conflict
counter-culture • Finances in marraige should be handled together to create unity

seven

MORE MONEY, MY MONEY, NO MONEY

Money is one of the most argued about topics in marriage today. According to a Citibank survey,[1] 57 percent of divorces result from disputes over money. However, if we dig a little deeper, it's not difficult to see that the issue really isn't about money at all, but how we approach life and our marriage.

There are three things that cause money to be an issue within our marriages: more money, my money and no money.

MORE MONEY
This first issue has more to do with our own individual greed and lack of contentment than actual marital problems. If needing to have "more money" is an issue in your marriage, it'll be an issue outside of your marriage. Like most of the problems in your marriage, just because you leave the marriage, doesn't mean you're leaving the problems. We might as well learn how to solve the problems within the marriage.

Being Content
God calls us to be content. Don't compare your current standard of living with your parents or your friends or your co-workers. Their seasons are different, what they went through to get to their current standard of living

is different, their purpose is different and you never truly know what's going on behind closed doors. You may want the car that someone else has right now, but do you want their financial crisis 3 years from now too? Comparing ourselves with anyone else is pointless. There will always be someone else that has something better than you in some way.

> *"Then I observed that most people are motivated to success because they envy their neighbors. But this too, is meaningless – like chasing the wind."*
> *–Ecclesiastes 4:4 (NLT)*

Be careful not to confuse contentment with complacency. Complacency is when you are so comfortable that you no longer desire to have anything beyond what you have right now. Contentment doesn't mean that we shouldn't have goals or aspirations in life. There's nothing wrong with wanting or appreciating a nicer house, newer car or better clothes. The problem comes when you want those things so much so that you become ungrateful for what you do have. Contentment is simply being grateful for what you have now and not needing anything more to make you feel satisfied or happy.

There was a YouTube video[2] (which was later turned into a meme) that is circulating on social media that brought this concept to life. We've added some dramatizations to this but the story goes something like this: Sitting at a red light is a beautiful exotic sports car. The guy sitting in the sports car sees a helicopter fly overhead and thinks to himself "I'd love to have a helicopter." Then a man with a newer SUV pulls up next to the sports car and he thinks to himself, "that's my dream car." Next, a lady in a new sedan crammed with kids, pulls up and sees the SUV and thinks, "I'd love to have a larger vehicle." Then a man pulls up with a decrepit car and clunks to a stop as his exhaust gives a loud pop. He looks over to the lady with the sedan and thinks to himself, "Look at that new car." Next to him, a bicyclist pedals his way to the stop light trying to balance himself with grocery bags hanging off both handlebars. He looks over at the decrepit vehicle and thinks to himself how convenient it would be to have a car at all, just somewhere he could load groceries into and use out of the elements. On the sidewalk next to the bicyclist, a girl walks up to the bus stop and sees the bike and thinks to herself how much faster she could get around if she had a bike. While the girl is waiting at the bus stop, a man in a wheelchair watches from a nearby balcony and thinks to himself, "she can go wherever she wants."

There is always something you have that someone else would be immensely grateful for. There will also always be something someone else has that you will want, no matter how much money you have. Not all things in life that are desirable can be bought with money. We have to learn to live within our means and be thankful and content with what we have.

It's foolish to want something so badly that we put more important aspects of our life - like our bills or food on the table - in jeopardy. We need to be objective in making decisions and keep our emotional desire for material goods on a leash. And yet, as foolish as it is to say it, how many of us make these "foolish" decisions on a regular basis? We've all been guilty of such foolish decisions.

The American Dream
Culture has created a distraction called the "American Dream". The brand-new home with a two-car garage in the neighborhood with the tennis courts and resort-style pool. If we aren't careful, that "American Dream" can very quickly cause us to lose sight of God's dream for our life.

God has called us to so much more than living in our perfect little house with our perfect little family and living out our days in peace and harmony amongst ourselves. He's called us to reach a lost and dying world. But for some of us, we're so wrapped up in mortgages and expenses that we are forced to keep a job we don't believe God has called us to so we can maintain the "American Dream" standard.

When you look at the origin of the word "mortgage" you find that "mort" means "death" and "gage" means "grip". So essentially, "mortgage" means "death grip". We're certainly not suggesting that no one ever have a mortgage. We're just trying to expose the significance of the mindset that our culture lives in. Culturally, it's not the dream to be content with just enough material possessions, to have influence and to love people. Culturally, it's the dream to have as many material possessions as you can, even if it means that you end up selling your soul in a death grip that you can't escape from.

In the vast majority of cases for the average American, the world's standard for prosperity isn't real prosperity, it's only a perceived prosperity. Someone may have a brand-new car, nice clothes, a huge house, designer purses and Rolex watches but they may also have a car payment they can't afford, out-of-control credit card debt and a house that looks nice but lack the funds to maintain or repair it. None of those things (house, car, clothes) are bad but we need to learn to be content with what we have and allow God to open the doors for more in His timing. Perhaps God promised us a mansion in Heaven so we would stop lusting after one on Earth.

We have to change our perspective. We are not called to live according to the world's standard, but to God's standard.

I (Gloria) don't tend to be into the name brand items. Whether that was because I could never afford them or because I legitimately didn't care, I'm not sure. But a few years ago, my mom gave me a really cute little Coach purse. I was so excited! I coordinated it with an outfit that I planned to wear to church the following Sunday. As I got out of my car, I walked into the church with my Coach purse hanging off my shoulder. I had a little bit of an extra bounce in my step, my shoulders were pulled back further and my head held a little bit higher. I have to admit, it surprised me. I always heard other people say that having nice, name-brand items made them feel more confident, but I had never experienced it myself. Then, mid-stride, I heard God ask me a question. Not audibly, but in my thoughts, this question interrupted my confident walk down the hallway. "Why does having a Coach purse hanging off your shoulder make you feel so much more confident?" Well, after I really analyzed it, it made me feel like I had something special that most people didn't have, which ultimately made me feel like I was better or more special than they were; therefore, I felt more confident. It was a revelation for me. Did I believe that God would condone such thinking? Was it Christ-like for me to have something because it made me feel like I was better than other people? Then I realized that my motivation for wanting a Coach purse wasn't Biblical. Having a Coach purse wasn't unbiblical, but my motivation for wanting a Coach purse was unbiblical. So I said thank you, gave the Coach purse back and went back to my purse-less existence (which is so much more convenient for me).

I'm not saying that everyone should go and burn all their Coach purses and Rolex watches. Please hear what I'm saying. Sometimes, people prefer those items because they are a higher quality product with better features or it was a gift. Sometimes, having a name-brand item is simply a method that allows a Christian to be accepted and relatable to a specific class of people – a class that also needs to hear about the love of Jesus. As much as we want to preach equality and universal acceptance, the sociological truth is, it's much easier for people to readily accept information or a call to Christ from someone that they feel understands them or relates to them. That's true for most everyone. So in that context, sometimes Coach purses, Rolex watches and Lexus cars are simply an accepted part of a culture that a specific group of people live in. A group you may be called to reach.

Every individual and situation is different. My point is not that you completely abandon all forms of material excess in your life and aren't allowed to enjoy the things that God has blessed you with. My point is that I think it is wise for us to examine our motivation behind wanting something materially and examine whether or not that motivation draws us closer to God or distracts us from God. It is healthy to live in the tension of whether something is perfectly acceptable or going too far. It's not that we can't have nice things at all, but we can't allow ourselves to become focused or distracted by the nice things.

"The seed cast in the weeds represents the ones who hear the kingdom news but are overwhelmed with worries about all the things they have to do and all the things they want to get. The stress strangles what they heard, and nothing comes of it."
—Mark 4:19 (MSG)

Money is not God

Finally, our dependence should be on God. When we use spending as a way to cope with our emotional needs, we are making money our God. This is true for anything we do therapeutically in place of going to God.

Money is a resource that God gives us to provide for us what we need, to be able to give to others and to bless us. We must be good stewards with that resource. Buying something extra for ourselves or our kids every time we walk into any store or going shopping when we are bored or depressed, is not a wise way to spend that resource.

Exercising greater self-control in our shopping habits, growing closer to God in our dependency when we need a mood lift, not getting wrapped up in the things of this world and being grateful for what we have, are all ways that we can diminish the power of needing to have more money and consequently, reduce the chances of money becoming an issue in our marriages.

MY MONEY

It's a popular trend these days for each spouse to have their own financial accounts, split the bills equally or take turns paying for things. It seems like a fair and streamlined method to handle finances - the husband pays his portion of the bills and if he wants to buy something, he can do so with what's leftover in his budget and vice versa.

However, what this creates is a culture in your marriage of dividing things up, 50/50, being fair, looking out for #1 (i.e. yourself) or placing yourself in a position of judgment towards your spouse if ever they aren't able to hold up their end of the deal. Not to mention the complete overhauling of the God-ordained roles in marriage – after all, if each person is responsible for their own actions individually and suffers their own consequences individually, there is no need to have a collaborative relationship. It eliminates the fighting in the marriage because it eliminates the merging of two individuals in a marriage and therefore eliminates any growth through your marriage. At the end of the day, the absence of fighting won't negate the feeling of being "on your own" even within your marriage and keeping your finances separate just makes it exponentially easier to simply walk away – which is good, if you got married with the intention of getting divorced. But we'd like to believe that most people reading this book got married with the intention of having a happily ever after, together.

God intended for you and your spouse to be one flesh. Money is not so important that it is above this fact. Marriage is not about dividing things up, it's about joining things together so much so that you can't tell what belongs to one person or the other. Marriage is not about splitting things up 50/50, it's about putting in 100% even when the other person puts in nothing. Marriage is not about being fair, it's about being self-sacrificing. Marriage is not about looking out for your well-being, it's about looking out for your spouse's well-being. It's not about placing yourself on the throne of judgment but having the opportunity to extend Grace and show God's love continuously.

If this is what God intended for our marriages, then how can we justify handling any aspect of our lives, including our money, any differently? Just like you tithe your first fruits out of obedience to represent that money is not your god nor your provider, but that only God is God, so it is with how you handle your money in your marriage – it is a good indicator of how you and your spouse approach your marriage.

So keep it together. There should be no "your money, my money, your bills, my bills". This eventually leads to "your friends, my friends, your job, my job, your life, my life, etc."

Now, that's not to say that there aren't good, legitimate reasons to have separate bank accounts or items in just your name or your spouse's name. There are countless situations that may mandate such separation. However, whether your money is in joint or separate accounts is not as important as both of you being aware of and managing all those financial accounts together, regardless of who's name they are in.

Commit to Commitment

As mentioned earlier, our assumption is that you did not get married with the intention of getting divorced. Yet, it is common advice for women, especially, to have a "back-up" plan, a secret account – just in case things go south. However, if you have no "back-up plan" to leave your marriage, then you are forced by the lack of options to stay with your spouse and find a way to work it out. Which is the point.

I (Gloria) can't tell you how many times during the toughest seasons of our marriage I toyed with the idea of leaving "for a while" just to get a break from Robert. I thought about where I could go. Getting a hotel room wasn't a viable financial option. And my mom had made it clear several times that if I ever wanted to leave Robert, that staying at her house would not be an option because I made a commitment to stay with him forever and she wasn't going to give me an easy way out when things got tough. Whether she's correct in her approach or not, I can tell you that her removing the option to move back in with my parents has successfully prevented me from attempting to leave Robert on several occasions – because I had no convenient place to go.

Sometimes when we talk about "committing" to marriage, we don't realize what the word "commit" truly means. It doesn't mean "try out" the marriage and see how it goes. It means, you're committed, no matter what. By setting yourself up with an escape plan, you are self-sabotaging, because when the going gets tough, you'll always know in the back of your mind, that leaving is an option. Prepare for a great marriage, not for an easy divorce.

"So then, they are no longer two but one flesh.
Therefore what God has joined together, let not man separate."
—Matthew 19:6 (NKJV)

Accept your Role

As discussed in chapters 3 (Dictators) and 4 (Doormats), there shouldn't be a power struggle in a Biblical marriage. A husband should love his wife so much that he sacrificially makes decisions in her best-interest. A wife, regardless if her husband is doing his part, should respect her husband's decision.

Marriage is a relationship of mutual respect and mutual submission. However, when it comes down to it, God has given the decision-making authority to the husband, even if he makes the wrong decision.

If you are separating finances to avoid a power struggle of who gets to spend what money and who's responsible for paying what, then you are just putting a band-aid on an issue that will manifest in other parts of your marriage.

The person who brings home the money doesn't get exclusive decision-making power for what happens with that money. Money belongs to the marriage and decisions should be decided accordingly – with the husband having vetoing power.

No Secrets

There are many smaller benefits to managing your money together. Having separately managed accounts makes it too easy to hide expenses for activity that your spouse would not agree with. Managing finances together, automatically creates an environment of accountability and honesty. When your spouse is aware of where money is being spent, then you are less likely to make the wrong choices and your spouse is given the opportunity to hold you accountable.

Separate, secret accounts only serve to encourage secret activity and a lack of communication. It opens the door to secret spending, secret purchases (porn, overspending, casual lunches with a "friend", etc.). There should be no secrets. Each of your financial accounts should be an open book available to each other.

Work Together

Life is full of conflicts. The goal in our marriage is not to learn how to avoid all conflict. The goal is to learn how to work together as a team to resolve conflict. Going through the process of learning how to manage your finances together, in unity, provides the valuable opportunity for each of you to grow as individuals and in your marriage. Welcome the opportunity. It's not always easy, but if you keep walking in the right direction, eventually, all the little hiccups in your marriage will be non-issues and you'll be able to redirect your focus on reaching the world instead of just struggling with your marriage.

NO MONEY

Now we come to the not so fun part of finances – the seasons when you have no money. Those seasons are some of the toughest, especially when you have children to care for. Unfortunately, when both spouses are at their wit's end and solutions don't seem to be in existence, we do the only thing we know to do – blame our spouse. It's not that we are hateful people, but it's a natural tendency for human beings to want to find a solution when faced with a problem. The only way to find a solution, is to point out the problem. But the reality is, sometimes we go through tough seasons, and although you or your spouse may have made mistakes, the entirety of the situation you are going through is rarely just one person's fault.

Robert and I (Gloria) used to joke that we never had any money problems – because in order to have money problems, you have to have money. And we had none. For about the first decade of our marriage, we lived in one financial crisis after another. When we first got married, we had 6-months of financial stability. Then I was unexpectedly laid-off due to downsizing. It was during this season that we would walk into Walmart with a $20 bill that was supposed to last us the entire week. Ramen noodles are already my favorite food, so that wasn't a problem. But we quickly learned how to maximize our meal options with limited ingredients. Like the best ways to make pizza out of a package of pepperonis and sandwich bread – but no cheese, we couldn't afford cheese. Through all the tears and prayers, we survived and God provided me with another great job.

Then shortly afterward, Robert was laid-off after a company merger rendered his position unneeded and we went through the whole cycle again. Robert and I are both entrepreneurial visionaries, so after months of jobless interviews, we decided to open up a chain of cell phone stores. Then we lost those stores when AT&T bought out Cingular. He got another great job, which moved us to a different city. Then the recession happened in 2008 and Robert was laid-off when the bank he worked for cut the workforce in half and laid people off according to their hire date. After months of more unproductive job interviews, including one as a pizza delivery man, Robert went into real estate - during the recession. He actually did bizarrely well and we were able to get back on our feet his first few months and then nothing.

He finally got a 9-5 job and we were doing well for several months - until that company nearly went out of business due to losing their contract with a company who produced 60% of their workload and Robert was laid-off in the process. Sometime during those years of business losses and lay-offs, Robert was called into ministry and the rest is history.

I don't want to make it all sound bad. We definitely had seasons of living the "high-life". At almost every job, Robert was always one of the highest-grossing employees and for at least two of those seasons, we brought home a comfortable six-figure income. But this only served to help us catch-up, build-up savings, get laid-off and stay jobless until every account we had was depleted and start over again. It was a vicious cycle that included all the stresses that come along with having no money.

In hindsight, Robert and I wouldn't change a thing. It was through those devastating seasons that we learned to grow closer to God, closer to each other, grow in our character and realize the calling on our lives. It seems weird to say it, but now, we view those seasons as a blessing - not only for the growth we experienced in our lives, but because it gave us experience and credibility in relating to other people. It gives us a bridge to help other people who are struggling with very real scenarios.

It's through our own experiences, that we learned the following five truths that we hope will encourage you if you are going through a similar season of "no money."

Tithe

Without tithing, there is no guarantee of God's provision. When you step out of God's will, it doesn't mean that you will always fail, but it does mean that all bets are off. The financial security that God promises to those who tithe will not be available to you. That doesn't mean that God will provide for every immediate bill or come up with a way for you to keep your house. But it does mean that He will provide for your basic needs and He will be faithful in blessing you in the big-scheme of your life. If we can trust God to save us when we die, then we can trust Him to save us when we need food on the table.

Trust

Every financial crisis you go through is an opportunity for growth. Sometimes we make bad financial decisions and suffer the consequences. Sometimes our financial crisis is the result of a legitimate attack from the enemy. But sometimes, what we see as a season of devastation, is actually a season that God is using to wean our souls of everything we depend on outside of God so that we can hear His voice more clearly and follow Him to the destiny He has called us to.

We have to learn to trust God. Trust that He can give us a second-chance and show us how to make better decisions. Trust that He can deliver us from an attack. And trust that even though the only thing we can see is the chaos all around us, He sees the bigger picture and has a bigger purpose and He knows how to show up at the right time with the right resources.

Encourage Each Other

Especially in a time of crisis, don't place blame but continually encourage each other. We always have two choices in our relationship with our spouse during trials: we can put them down, demean them, blame them and position ourselves opposed to them or we can position ourselves beside them, constantly encouraging them, reaffirming them and lifting them up.

I'm reminded of the story in Exodus 17. The Israelites were engaged in battle and Moses stood on a mountaintop holding his hands up. As he grew tired and started lowering his hands, the Israelites would begin to lose. But when he lifted his hands back up, the Israelites would begin to defeat their enemy again. Aaron and Hur were with him. When they saw that Moses was growing tired during the battle and began dropping his hands, they could have yelled at him for being selfish or not trying hard enough. After all, thousands of men were on the battlefield risking their lives and all Moses had to do to save them was keep his hands raised. Aaron and Hur could have hurled insults at him about his age or his pride or his carelessness or how he should have prepared better for that day and did more push-ups so he could keep his arms up. While he was being worn down physically, they could have worn him down emotionally as well. But they didn't. Instead, "Aaron and Hur held his hands up – one on one side, one on the other – that his hands remained steady till sunset" (Exodus 17:12 NIV). They were all in the battle together. They could have turned on each other, but they encouraged each other.

The same is true in our marriages. Your spouse does not desire to fail at life. They do not desire to be broke, stressed and depressed. They do not desire to feel hopeless or disappoint their family. And yet, during times of trial, especially when pertaining to "no money" seasons, this is how you and your spouse probably feel. Instead of compounding the situation and turning on each other, remember that you are both going through the trial.

Regardless of who is at fault, you are both suffering and you both want a solution that doesn't seem to be on the horizon. When your spouse is down, lift them up and when you are feeling discouraged, your spouse should encourage you. You are on the same side. Don't let the enemy use your circumstances to cause your marriage to crumble from within.

Share your Thoughts

Share your thoughts. Don't hide how you feel, allow your spouse the opportunity to encourage you. Especially men. Husbands need to be honest with their wives. If you aren't willing to share, your wife may not realize how tough the "no money" season is on you.

I (Gloria) know that during our "no money" seasons, I was so consumed with my own discouragement and depression that I never stopped to think how Robert felt. I knew that he was struggling like I was, but it wasn't until he opened up about his feelings of failure and inadequacy that I realized just how much of his identity was wrapped up in his ability to provide for his family. He was taking it harder than I was, he just didn't express himself the same way I did. When I finally realized what he was going through, it gave me the opportunity to encourage him on how great of a husband he was and how good he was to me and how God would use this for His glory one day. But such things can't happen if you don't share what you are going through.

Every Season Passes

Finally, remember that every season passes. You will not live in this season forever. Sure, it may be several years, a decade even, but it will eventually pass. No season is permanent and God will do miraculous things with that season that will eventually make you even, dare I say it, glad to have gone through those horrible "no money" times.

KEEP YOUR EYES ON THE PRIZE

Whether you have "more money" than you know what to do with or are holding tight to "my money" or going through a season of "no money", remember that money is not your God, it's not your provider and it's not what makes your marriage work or not work. Take your eyes off the money aspects of your life and focus on God and He'll provide exactly what you need.

PROVING PRIORITIES PRACTICALLY

#priorities

culture • Life is too busy to make time for things that are not immediately demanded
counter-culture • Life is too short to allow only what's demanded to dictate your time

eight

PROVING PRIORITIES PRACTICALLY

Think through these questions: What are your priorities in life? God? Family? Sports? Fun? Cleaning? Keeping up appearances?

Now think through these: What do you think about the most? What influences your decisions the most? What do you stress out about the most on a day-to-day basis?

Based on the answers to the latter three questions, what do you think other people would say your priorities are?

We can claim that something is our priority until we are blue in the face, but if our behaviors do not indicate that something is a priority, then it's not a genuine priority. What you say is nowhere near as effective as what you do.

FIRST THINGS FIRST
The priorities that you demonstrate will define you: who you live for, who you are and what you do. As Christians, we understand that God is our top priority. Your personal relationship with God should not only be your top priority, but an all-consuming priority that takes precedence over all other priorities. But what does that mean?

The majority of people correlate time with priority level. So naturally, if someone says God should be your biggest priority in life, then you may be tempted to say that the "super spiritual" people who are doing it right are spending the bulk of their day in prayer, Bible reading and in church. But spending the bulk of our time each day with God means that there are not enough hours in the day to fulfill what is important to God Himself. He calls us to love our neighbor, to care for the widows and fatherless, to raise our children – and all of these things take time. So how do we do both?

Demonstrating that God is your priority doesn't necessarily mean that you allocate the majority of your day to only spending personal time with God. He's your first priority, yes. But simply getting up each morning and devoting 30 minutes to reading your Bible and then proceeding with your day according to your own will, does not mean that you are making Him your first priority. He's an all-consuming priority. Which means that everything you do throughout your entire day, every person you encounter, how you handle every situation, what you spend your money on – every action you make the entire day should indicate that God is your top priority.

This doesn't necessarily mean that you spout off scripture with every encounter you have with every person or that you go through all the motions of religious activity without error. It means that your personal and intimate relationship with God goes beyond the religious expectations of the church. That even your hidden thoughts demonstrate that God is your top priority.

LOVE THY NEIGHBOR

> *"Jesus replied: 'Love the Lord your God with all your heart and with all your soul and with all your mind. This is the first and greatest commandment. And the second is like it: Love your neighbor as yourself. All the Law and the Prophets hang on these two commandments.'"*
> *-Matthew 22:37-40 (NIV)*

Your spouse is the closest "neighbor" you have and great time should be devoted to loving and caring for them. If God is our priority, then we need to understand what's important to Him and make that a priority. If God says that He "hates divorce" (Malachi 2:16), then subsequently, we need to decide that caring for our marriage and our spouse is a priority.

It means that when you have to choose between your emotions and your marriage – you make your marriage your priority, not your emotions. When you have to choose between leaving and giving yourself a fresh start or rolling up your sleeves and digging into some pretty nasty dirt to work through your marital issues – you choose not to take the easy way out. If God is our priority, then that means our spouses are our priorities and whatever it takes to stand by our spouse is the option we should choose.

ALL MY CHILDREN

"Deacons must be husbands of only one wife,
and good managers of their children and their own households."
-1 Timothy 3:12 (NASB)

I Timothy gives us a good outline of how priorities should line up with our families: spouse, children, household. It is through demonstrating that God and your spouse are your priorities that we indirectly make our children a top priority. There is nothing greater you can give your children than a great example of how they should live their lives.

It's popular culture that children are placed as a higher priority than spouses and understandably so. There is an overwhelming sense of responsibility and ownership and of course, love, when you are given the opportunity to develop a human being. Combine that love and responsibility with the fact that children naturally need more care than an adult and it's easy to see how our priorities can shift from our marriages to our children.

However, the greatest gift we can give our children is a front row-seat to witness how life should be lived, how decisions should be made, what commitment looks like and how God can hold it all together. It's in the foundational years of their development that their perspective on God, life and relationships is ingrained into their souls. We make our children our top priority by showing them, by example, how to make God their top priority.

PEOPLE AROUND THE WORLD

God loves people. We should love people. After we have taken care of the people that God has given us exclusive responsibility over (our spouse, our children and our household), then it should be our priority to love other people. No matter our vocation or our calling, God has called us to ultimately love people. Whether that be through volunteer ministry, our relationship with colleagues or caring for extended family – we should make loving and caring for people a part of our daily existence.

Within the first several years of our marriage, Robert's stepfather died a tragic death after a steep emotional and mental decline. Never having met his biological father, Robert's stepfather was, by all intents and purposes, his dad. During the season before his death, when he had disconnected from the family, I (Gloria) felt a constant nudge to write Robert's dad a letter. I don't know what was supposed to be in the letter other than a few words of encouragement and acceptance. Although Robert and his dad were close, I really didn't have a relationship with him beyond father-in-law/daughter-in-law status, so the idea of writing him a letter seemed a little bizarre. I consistently pushed the thought away in favor of tending to my fast-paced productive life – after all, I'm a huge fan of productivity.

Several months after his death, I merged my Outlook contact list into my Gmail contact list and was taking the time to delete duplicates, categorize each contact and update everyone's information – because that's what I do for fun (no, seriously). As I was scrolling the long list of names, I came upon Robert's dad's name: Paul Brundage. I stopped for a moment and for whatever reason, instead of just deleting the contact, I opened it up to review the information I had under his name – reflecting on the entire situation again.

In Outlook, a "priority" setting was assigned to every contact by default. As I scrolled to the bottom of Paul Brundage's information, I saw the last field of information: "Priority: Low". "Priority: Low". That's it. I know that the software assigned all my contacts with a "Priority: Low" status, but it still hit me like a ton of bricks. My heart sank and, in that moment, God broke me. Two simple words that God used to give me a revelation of how messed up my priorities were.

In a season when God called me to extend love and grace to someone, I had demonstrated that my to-do list was a higher priority than people. My work, my own little world, my own little responsibilities were more important than taking ten minutes to provide what could have been a life-altering extension of God's love in someone's life. I'm not saying that my little note would've saved Robert's dad's life, but we'll never know how God intended to work if my priorities would've lined up with God's priorities. I claimed that God was my first priority, but in that situation, I proved that what was important to God, was not important to me.

God works through interruptions to show people His love. Although we need to be faithful with the task that God has given us – to do it diligently and with excellence – we absolutely cannot allow what we are doing to keep us from extending love toward people.

Danny Silk put it so concisely when he said "If you love me, it is going to show up in the way you treat what I told you is important to me. If we truly love God it should show in the way we treat what He has told us in His Word is important to Him."

WORKING ALL DAY LONG

Finally, we get to the final priority in our list of top five priorities: your assigned task. Whether that be a 9-5 job, a student or a calling, your "task" is what you do.

Notice that what you do comes after people. Meaning, "work" doesn't come before your family. It also means that ministry work (employed or volunteer) doesn't go before family either. Your personal relationship with God and ministry work are two separate priority listings.

With nearly all things in life, we can create lists and draw lines and boundaries to give us some kind of clarity, but we also have to learn to apply balance and wisdom. God takes us through seasons and sometimes circumstances dictate that we may have to choose going to work from 9-5 instead of staying at home playing with the kids all day or we may have to forego one marriage retreat in order to pay for a mission trip.

The idea is not that we always have to choose a higher priority instead of a lower priority in every circumstance. The idea is that we are living in balance and we live with an understanding that it is how we handle our priorities on a day-to-day basis and the overall health of our priorities that we need to be aware of.

PRACTICING YOUR PRIORITIES

All this talk of what our priorities should be is great – but what really matters is how we apply that to our lives. Proving our priorities is a very different matter than being able to list our priorities.

Prioritizing Priorities

The first thing we need to be able to do is prioritize our priorities. If something is a priority then make it a priority to find time for that priority. If something is a priority in your life, you tend to it. When it's a real priority, we don't just forget about it. We wouldn't leave our kids at school without a ride. As a married couple, we have to remember that just because something isn't important to us, doesn't mean that it's not important for our spouse. If it's a priority for our spouse within our marriage, then we have to make it a priority for ourselves.

Like we covered earlier, there are the occasional circumstances that dictate that we may have to allocate time to something else instead of time with our spouse. However, that's the exception, not the norm.

Learn your priority's priorities. What is important to your spouse? What do they need from you in order to feel that you have a successful marriage? Whatever their answers are may seem trivial to you, but if your spouse is a priority, then make what is important to them, important to you as well.

Make Adjustments

Once you understand what is important to your spouse, then evaluate how you run your life. Aside from the occasional exception, if your actions regularly and by default reduce your spouse down the priority list, then it's time to make some adjustments. Make logistical changes to your life in order to develop a lifestyle around your priorities.

Are you making adjustments in your life so that your spouse's priorities make it on your task list for the day? We'll cover this more later in this chapter, but for example, if sex is a priority for your spouse - no matter how superficial you may think it is - are you making sure that you are setting aside time and energy for yourself to be able to make sex a priority in your life as well?

Naturally, if something is important to you, you don't need reminders or changes to your life – you'll make sure you do what you feel is important. However, if something is important to your spouse, you'll need to take the extra steps to set up reminders or make adjustments to your schedule to demonstrate that what's important to your spouse, is important to you.

In my (Robert) supporting role at a quickly expanding international ministry, I have found that the vast majority of my time is quickly consumed by ministry work. Every decision I make in ministry is dependent on God's Will and my personal relationship with God maintains its place of priority in my life (Priority #1), it is what God has called me to do (Priority #5) and through my position I make a conscious effort to make it a priority to love people and not get carried away with being task-driven (Priority #4). The priorities that slowly began to regularly get less of my time were my spouse (Priority #2) and my children (Priority #3).

Realizing that no matter our heart or our intent, that ministries and callings crumble quickly when we do not stay balanced in our priorities, Gloria and I found ways to make logistical changes to our lifestyle. Whereas in previous seasons of my life, I rarely missed a football game; in the current season of my life, football games have been replaced with date nights. Because of a heavier ministry commitment, I wasn't able to make it home and do family outings as often as my family would prefer, so we stopped making family outings and date nights separate entities from our ministry calling. After all, ministry is a family affair. Instead of me going out of town to a different campus to work, my family went with me and we made it a family road trip. Instead of me working on an event on my own, Gloria volunteered right beside me. This worked for us because for Gloria, work is what she does for fun, productivity is important to her. Being able to work together and be productive collaboratively was the ultimate expression of marital health. On top of merging ministry and family where doable, we also decided to take as many vacations as possible – thankfully, Gloria's parents live on the beach, so taking multiple vacations wasn't a financial stretch for us. With the combination of including my family in my work and setting aside several opportunities throughout the year for exclusive family time, Gloria and our children were reestablished in their right place in my list of priorities.

As seasons change, the logistics of how we do life may change. The adjustments we made in our life may not work for you and your spouse – you may not be able to include them in your work, or your wife may not consider working together a fulfilling outlet for your marriage or vacations may not be as doable as setting aside nearly every Saturday night as a "family night". What works for us may not work for you and your spouse, but the idea is that you're constantly evaluating your priorities against the current season you are in and communicating with each other on solutions that will prove to your priority that they are actually the priority.

Balance Your Priorities

We feel the most important aspect to juggling life commitments is balance and wisdom. I know that we keep going back to this but we cannot stress it enough. The last thing we want is for someone to take the content in this book and rigidly apply it to their lives with no regards to balance and wisdom. There are scriptural guidelines that cannot be compromised, but outside of those, we have to pray for wisdom to be able to discern when guidelines can be adjusted for a specific situation.

For instance, my (Gloria) job in the film industry is largely project-based. For the majority of the year I am able to work from home while the kids are at school or during their naps. Then when my family is home, I try to focus exclusively on them. With that being said, there are times that I'll need to be away for a week or occasionally several weeks at a time during production or I'll need to be completely focused on pre-production responsibilities leading up to a shoot. These occasions occur one or two times throughout the year and Robert understands that the shift in priorities is temporary and has an end date.

On the other hand, there have also been occasions when I had the opportunity to take back-to-back projects that I had to decline. This is where discernment and God's direction weighed heavily in our decisions. It's one thing to need to focus on my work for a heavy deadline but have the ability to "make-up" for it the remainder of the year by being present at home. It's an entirely different scenario if it becomes normal to have one heavy deadline after another with no end in sight and no ordination directly from God to take the extra workload. When that happens, it becomes an issue of a permanent priority shift vs. a temporary seasonal shift.

The Love Bucket

Have you heard of a love bucket? It's a concept that says that everyone has a bucket of things that they desire in order to feel fulfilled and loved and every time a significant other does one of those things, they fill up the love bucket – and the love bucket constantly has to be refilled.

Instead of a love bucket, let's call it a priority bucket. It's your responsibility to always keep your spouse's priority bucket full. Every time you choose your spouse or what is important to your spouse over something else, you are depositing into their priority bucket. But every time you choose something else – work, football, cleaning, even kids – over your spouse, you are withdrawing from their priority bucket. There are times when you need to make a withdraw from your spouse's priority bucket, but if you do so, remember that you need to find ways to make several deposits to fill it back up again. If your spouse's priority bucket goes empty and stays empty for too long, that's when you may need to take drastic measures to make sure your account stays in good standing.

GETTING PRACTICAL

We've listed out our priorities, we've discussed how to demonstrate our priorities, now we want to give you some real-life ways to prove your priorities practically. These examples do not cover every scenario by any means, but hopefully it'll give you a good grasp of how to apply this chapter to your life on a regular basis.

Sex vs. Sleep

Whatever your excuse, make adjustments to your schedule or set reminders for yourself. If it's important to your spouse, it should be important to you. If you are legitimately completely and totally drained by the time you get in the bed, then when you are contemplating whether or not to finish the laundry before you go to bed or go ahead and go to bed with some energy still reserved – choose to let the laundry wait. We understand that may be difficult to do mentally, but you have to ask yourself: What's my priority here? To have all my chores done successfully for the day and the house clean before I go to bed or is my spouse my priority? As already discussed earlier in the chapter, spouse is Priority #2 and your assigned task only comes in at Priority #5. If you are unsure as to which one is more important to your spouse, ask them: clean underwear or sex? And go from there.

Conversations vs. Relaxation

Whether you feel like talking or vegging out on the couch, if it's important to your spouse to connect with you on a daily basis, then reserve some energy throughout your day to do so. I (Robert) used to get so frustrated when I walked in the door from a chaotic day at work and the first thing Gloria wanted to do was talk about all the menial, tedious, boring things I did all day – what flavor coffee did I choose that morning? How did the conversation with my boss go (i.e. give her the transcript of the entire conversation verbatim)? What did I order for lunch? How did I feel about such and such? The last thing I wanted to do was talk at all – I talked all day. I just wanted to sit on the couch in silence. I didn't want to have to report everything I did to someone as soon as I got home. But eventually I realized that it was important for her to feel like she was included in my day. Even if she wasn't with me all day, she wanted to know what I did and how I felt about everything I did. So instead of walking in the door and getting frustrated, I changed my mindset. I went ahead and added it to my mental calendar. Since it became something I expected to have to do when I got home, I had all day to prepare and it wasn't so frustrating. Connecting conversationally about the day I just had still isn't my favorite thing to do, but it makes Gloria feel connected to me - which leads to other forms of physical connection and I'm not opposed to that.

Appreciation vs. Perfection

Decide what's more important: a perfectly completed task or your spouse feeling appreciated when they attempt to "help out". If you haven't already heard, I (Gloria) love efficiency and productivity. So naturally, I operate all aspects of my life to reach the highest form of efficiency possible. This extends to my closet. Most organized people organize by color because it looks nice. But I have found this to be an inefficient practice as there would be several articles of clothing that went unworn and there was no way to filter them out. So I organize my closet by type (long-sleeved, short-sleeved, t-shirts) and then I place freshly cleaned clothes to the right-side of each section. When I need to find something to wear, I just review the options on the left-side of each section. This way, when it's time for spring cleaning (and summer, and fall, and winter cleaning), I can easily see what I didn't wear all season and get rid of it. As you can see, this is a very delicate system I have created. One day, Robert decided to be helpful and put away the laundry for me. When I walked into my closet that evening, I wanted to cry. Not because what he did was so sweet, but because in an instant, I had lost several months of tracking what I no longer wore. Robert had hung clothes up in the wrong sections and on the wrong sides. Of course, I could go back and pick out the pieces that I knew weren't put away correctly - but that would mean that I lost (gasp) 10-minutes of my time reorganizing that I could've have used doing something else. And even then, there was no guarantee that I wouldn't overlook an article of clothing that was misplaced. I'm sure you see how detrimental this was to my existence (extreme sarcasm). I got pretty upset, which was extremely discouraging to Robert. In a situation where he was going out of his way to make me a priority and do something sweet for me, he failed. Worse than him failing, I made him feel like he failed. I wanted him to do sweet things for me, but when he attempted to do it, I got mad at him because he didn't do it to my standards of crazy perfection. In a sense, I punished him for being nice to me. The results? He said he would never try to hang up my laundry again. Fast-forward several years later and he has attempted to hang the laundry up a couple times again. It's not always perfect, but I've had to take a step back and ask myself what my priority is: Is it more important for something eternally irrelevant to be done perfectly or is it more important that I change my attitude and show immense appreciation that I have a husband who is willing to go the extra mile to assist me? The answer is simple from the outside looking in, but sometimes we can get so carried away in the moment that we forget that our behavior proves how our priorities are aligned.

Changing vs. Staying Stubborn

Your spouse may love you just the way you are, but it is also OK to willingly change your behavior to make them happy. We know this statement isn't popular in today's culture and we've dedicated an entire chapter to it (Chapter 9: Expect Less, Appreciate More). This whole concept in today's culture about being who you are and not changing for anyone is simply unbiblical. Yes, be confident in who you are and no, you should never change to get someone to like you or accept you. However, we are all in dire need of growth and change throughout our entire lives and even biologically, we change several times throughout our lifetime. There is absolutely nothing wrong with directing how that change happens. If your spouse has a preference for long hair, then there's nothing wrong with you growing your hair out. You don't have to stand on some philosophical ground that says you should never have to change anything about yourself. Your spouse should love you no matter what, but you should be willing to change some things in order to please your spouse. For example, I (Gloria) used to (this is arguably past tense) have a tendency to be a little overdramatic. One night, our two dogs got into a fight and I put my hand out to pull them back and our bigger dog bit my hand. And when I say bit, I mean, I felt his tooth on my hand – but you wouldn't be able to tell by looking at it. I got all dramatic over it because Robert downplayed it so much and just looked at me like I was crazy. Which of course, led to an argument. But what was more important? That he caters to my over dramatization regarding everything in my life or that I take the opportunity to mature in that part of my personality? And yes, for those that are in total disagreement, you absolutely can change aspects of your personality. I'm happy to report that my knee-jerk reaction is no longer to scream and cry but rather to have a "calm, cool and collected" demeanor (for the most part) until my insides stop freaking out. It wasn't natural at first, but it's definitely a change that has worked to my benefit in not only my marriage, but in my parenting and professional life.

Old Family vs. Spouse

When you chose to marry your spouse, you chose to leave your previous family behind (in the "leave and cleave" sense); although you strive to continue to honor and respect them, your spouse must take priority.

We've all heard it said that "when you marry someone, you also marry their family". This is true, but only to an extent. The Bible makes it clear that when we marry our spouses, we begin a new family. It would be great if everyone in your extended families could be one big happy bunch of people. But that's not always the way it works out. Sometimes, your "old family" may start a battle with your spouse. Who is right or wrong is not the point and can be discussed behind closed doors. But when you are faced with the decision on who's side to defend, your spouse should always take priority. You and your spouse should always stay united against anyone else. There should be no earthly tie or loyalty stronger than your marriage.

> *"For this reason a man shall leave his father and his mother and be joined*
> *to his wife; and they shall become one flesh."*
> *—Genesis 2:24 (NASB)*

God's Timing vs. Your Timing: You may have a very different calling than what you are experiencing now, but if God is your all-consuming priority, then He desires to control your life and you must let Him. Whatever your circumstances, choosing between making something happen in your life on your own or choosing to wait on God's timing, is ultimately indicative of how your priorities stack up. When God is ready for something to happen in your life, He can make it happen – as long as you are staying focused on your relationship with Him and following His will.

COMMUNICATE YOUR PRIORITIES

What's important to your spouse? Without knowing what's important to your spouse, it's going to be difficult to demonstrate that they are your priority. We have to be willing to talk through these topics and get to know each other. Things change, circumstances change, people change – we have to keep talking so we can know who our spouse is today and what they find important.

Whatever your priority-related scenario, before you make a decision, ask yourself, "by making this decision, who am I making a priority?"

EXPECT LESS, APPRECIATE MORE

#expectations #appreciation

culture • Marriage is all about finding someone who loves you the way you are
counter-culture • Marriage is all about being someone who loves them the way they are

nine

EXPECT LESS, APPRECIATE MORE

We tend to live in a double-standard in our current culture. We expect perfection from our spouses yet give ourselves a lot of slack. We ask our spouse to change things about themselves, yet we have this attitude that we shouldn't have to change for anyone. We expect our spouses to appreciate every little thing we do, yet we usually don't go out of our way to show our spouses that we appreciate what they do. At its core, it all comes down to the human flaw of selfishness and as we attempt to wade through the ugly world of our own selfishness, hopefully we can come out on the other side expecting less of our spouses and appreciating more of them, instead of the other way around.

AVOIDING CHANGE

Be yourself. You're perfect just the way you are. Never change. Be true to yourself. Just do you. Don't change for anyone.

These types of phrases helped Gloria feel confident being herself during seasons of insecurity. But although these statements may be well-meaning, empowering and often true – many times, they are also used as a way for people to justify the reasons they shouldn't have to mature in an area of their life. Culture has taken statements meant to empower us and turned them into statements that hinder us from growth.

It's absolutely true that our spouses should love and accept us without requiring us to change, but that doesn't mean that we should never change. Perhaps if both spouses within a marriage approached their relationship with the goal of loving and accepting their spouse without expecting them to change, but with a willingness to change who they are for the betterment of their marriage, both spouses would meet somewhere blissfully in the middle.

Stop Making Excuses

Some people seem to have a knack for excuses. No matter the circumstance or the reason, their justification always has to do with some event or person beyond their control. The truth is, the vast majority of the time, excuses and placing blame are just ways for us to avoid owning up to something, apologizing and changing.

For instance, in my (Gloria) case, I have a mild tendency to be late (although Robert feels "mild" is an understatement). Robert will try to tell you that I'm always late to everything. But that's not the truth. I have managed to be on time on a few occasions over the course of my life - so you really can't say I'm "always" late. That just wouldn't be accurate. Nevertheless, I do have a tendency to be late. It's not because I'm lazy or I don't schedule things appropriately. Really, it's because I schedule things so well that I end up having 10-15 minutes of spare time before I really, truly have to be somewhere – and it seems like such a waste to be 10-15 minutes early when I could be using that time to be productive and get ahead on my workload. So you see, my list of excuses when I do show up late are perfectly legitimate - to me.

I never saw a need to change my lifestyle of lateness because I justified it with productivity. However, Robert (and everyone else) just saw a bag full of excuses and a total disregard for their time. Although I felt my excuses were valid, my excuses were my justification to not have to change. I've since realized that my lateness was something that I needed to change.

I had to put away my excuses, change my mindset and make decisions to willingly waste 10-15 minutes of my time by being early – or at least on time. It's not fun. It would be so much easier and more convenient for me to continue making excuses rather than actually change my attitude about the value of my time (and more importantly, other people's time) and change long-established habits. I'm still late sometimes, but I think most everyone in my little world would be grateful to Robert for pushing me to change that part of myself. After all, change is a sign of maturity.

Change is a Sign of Maturity

We all change. Even biologically, just about every cell, bone and organ in our body regenerates itself over the course of a few days or several years and is recreated from the foods that we eat[1]. Brings new meaning to the phrase "you are what you eat." You are, literally what you eat because you are constantly in a state of biological regeneration.

The same is true with your personality. You are constantly changing, adjusting and maturing as you go through life and learn from different experiences.

For instance, when our children were toddlers, they would often throw temper tantrums when they didn't get what they wanted. This usually only resulted in some tears; but occasionally got to the point of falling on the floor, kicking and yelling. We imagine that you don't throw yourself on the floor and cry when you don't get something you want, do you? Or at least, let's hope you don't. Most adults have learned that there are more effective ways to react to disappointments in life.

In a more complex scenario, most adults have clothes on - or at least the vast majority of adults do. We have learned that society deems it inappropriate to walk around in our underwear. Most of us understand that if we want to have food, we need money and in order to have money, we need to get a job and in order to get a job, we typically need to wear clothes. Even though being nude is the essence of being "true to yourself" and who you really are, we change how we present ourselves because we are mature enough to comprehend concepts beyond black and white.

We aren't perfect and without a willingness to change, we will never mature. Don't be so stubborn and set in who you think you are that you refuse to let God mold you into who He created you to be. Change is how God transforms us to be more like Christ and change is how He is able to use us to reach all that He has called us to be and do. In fact, change is exactly what God intends to do with each one of us. In Romans 12 we are told "do not be conformed to this world but be transformed by the renewing of your mind". You see, it is God's plan to change us as we commit ourselves to Him. And sometimes - perhaps a lot of times, he instigates that change through our spouses.

DON'T EXPECT CHANGE

Change is a good thing – a great thing – a necessary thing - a God thing. Change is not something to avoid. On the other hand, understand that God loving you "just the way you are" is a major cornerstone of Christianity.

God doesn't ask you to change anything about yourself and accepts you wholeheartedly with arms wide open just the way you are. Changing or fixing anything about yourself or your life doesn't make God love you more – or less. God loves us no matter what and we should extend that same type of love to our spouses – accepting and loving our spouses just the way they are without expecting or asking them to change in any way.

Expecting Less

Prior to us getting married, we went through several candid and grueling pre-marital counseling sessions. Many of the viewpoints the counselor shared with us were the complete opposite from what I (Gloria) believed at that time – although they are beliefs I hold as truth now.

During one particular session, the counselor looked at me and asked, "when you get married, what expectations do you have for Robert as a husband?" I thought about it for a moment, and responded "well, I expect him to be faithful to me and be a spiritual leader for me, to be obedient to God and be there for me..." The counselor responded, "and what would you do if he didn't do those things?" I quickly responded with "I don't know, I don't think he wouldn't do those things, that's the whole reason I'm marrying him."

At that, the counselor informed me that I needed to eliminate my expectations of Robert – that I should enter marriage without expecting him to do anything. I argued. Because that's what I tend to do. I completely missed what he was saying. I kept thinking to myself, "what in the world!?! So I should just marry him and not expect him to hold up his end of the bargain and let him do whatever he wants!?!" Exactly.

It sounds crazy. But our natural tendency is to enter into marriage with the expectation that our spouse will continue to be exactly who we think they are before we are married or be exactly who we expect them to be going into marriage. But what if they change for the worse? Or what if they don't change for the better? What if they fail to meet our expectations? What then? Do we call the marriage off? Do we sit sulking in the corner? Stuck in a marriage we didn't expect to have?

When we think of the standard marital vows, "for better or for worse" we tend to think of financial hardships or failing health or rough seasons. It's rare that we interpret the "worse" to mean that our spouse fails to be the quality of person we hoped they would be for the rest of their life.

We can hope that our spouse will be all the things we want them to be, but to expect them to meet our expectations is setting them and our marriage up for failure. It's basically making the statement, "I'm committed to you until you are no longer meeting my criteria."

But this is why marriages end – because we expect our spouses to be a certain way for our benefit and then when they're not – we call it off and end it. Marriage the way God intended doesn't work like that. It's a commitment. There is no way out – or there shouldn't be.

For some, using the phrase "there is no way out" sounds depressing or like it's a punishment. Just the contrary. It's the confirmation you might need to stand up, love your spouse, love yourself, love God and move forward making the best out of what you might have been viewing as a tough situation. You've heard the phrase "if you can't beat em', join em'. Well here's a new one: if you can't leave em', love em'.

You Can Only Change You

If you approach your marriage with the expectation that you can change your spouse, you will be disappointed on a daily basis. Your acceptance and love for your spouse should never be based on them meeting your standards or expectations.

You can only change you. If you are married, you are married no matter what your spouse does or does not become. You can't change them, nor should you expect them to change, nor should you withhold your love and acceptance of them because they don't change.

Only God can change them. God may use you to challenge them to grow or reveal areas in their life that needs to change; but ultimately, only God can truly change them. If you do somehow nag them to the point that they are forced to change, you didn't really change them, you just changed their behavior – and you probably made them bitter and resentful in the process. You've changed what they do, not why they do it. You've changed their behavior, you haven't changed their heart.

But God can change them and does change people with love and grace. Leave the transformation work to God. When He changes someone, it's not behavior modification - it's life transformation. It's not a change of mind - it's a change of heart.

Two Wrongs Don't Make a Right

What happens when we put expectations on our spouse and they don't meet them? If we've determined that they will never change and we then start to default on our part as a spouse, we are letting ourselves and our marriage down. Two wrongs do not make a right.

If you are excusing yourself from being a better husband/wife because your spouse is failing in some way, you are just as much to blame.

"You, therefore, have no excuse, you who pass judgement on someone else,
for at whatever point you judge another, you are condemning yourself,
because you who pass judgement do the same things."
-Romans 2:1 (NIV)

Whether you are withholding your responsibilities as a Godly husband or wife or blaming your spouse for their failures, you are just as much in the wrong as your spouse.

You made a commitment to your spouse. Even if they don't hold up their end of the bargain, that does not excuse you from holding up yours or give you permission to "punish" your spouse in some way. Allow God the opportunity to intervene and handle things in His timing and methods. You are responsible for your own actions, not your spouses. If you try taking action into your own hands and attempt to correct your spouse, you are only delaying God's opportunity to work on your spouse. You're getting in the way. Step back, examine yourself, love your spouse and let God work on each of you.

"Do not take revenge, my dear friends, but leave room for God's wrath, for
it is written: 'It is mine to avenge; I will repay,' says the Lord."
-Romans 12:19 (NIV)

You may not be "punishing" or withholding love from your spouse because they aren't meeting your expectations, but are you blaming them for your failures? Are you using them as an excuse for your own actions instead of taking responsibility?

For example, maybe you and your spouse are having financial struggles and your response is "if you did a better job taking care of the family and cooking then we wouldn't have to spend money on going out all the time!" Or maybe you feel that you haven't reached your full potential in life or don't have the confidence to take hold of big opportunities and you think to yourself, "if my spouse was more supportive, I could go after my dreams." These statements may hold some truth in them. But only partially. Don't use your spouse as an excuse for your setbacks.

Sometimes, it's easier for us to find someone else to blame than to put the effort into changing ourselves or how we manage our lives. But these excuses further reinforce that two wrongs do not make a right.

When I (Robert) first started to focus on getting to optimum health, I made a diligent effort to find time to run or go to the gym. I wanted to be in shape. But there were times that I felt that Gloria was working against me. She'd call and ask if I wanted to have lunch with her during a break that I would've gone to the gym. Or when I got home, she'd ask for help around the house - making a run around the neighborhood too complicated to find time for in the evenings. Days or weeks would go by when I missed workouts. Gloria would ask, "I thought you were trying to get into shape?" To which I quickly replied, "I am, but you're sabotaging me." It's an easy excuse. And although having her support would've greatly increased my ability to get in shape, there were things that I could've done to make sure I got workouts in. I could've woken up an hour earlier, I could've turned down the lunch date and saved money and went for a workout instead (but who wants to eat a salad in the office when they could go out with their beautiful wife for lunch?) I could've ran after we put the kids to bed instead of plopping myself down on the couch.

The truth is, as much as I wanted to blame Gloria for her lack of logistical support in the health and fitness area of my life, I was just as much to blame and I had to take responsibility for my own choices and decisions.

Instead of trying to balance our spouse's wrong with a wrong of our own,

God calls us to be long-suffering. If our spouse doesn't behave the way we desire, we should continue to serve them as the husband/wife God has called us to be with even greater fervency. Galatians 6:9-10 says "Let us not become weary in doing good, for at the proper time we will reap a harvest if we do not give up." We're not saying that it's easy when your spouse doesn't meet your expectations or if they seem to be fighting against you. But we are saying that being patient with them and continuing to love them and be committed to them is what God calls us to do and through that, it will be far easier for your spouse to be receptive of the transformation that God may be taking them through.

Our Spouse Cannot Be God for Us

Your spouse cannot be God for you. Sometimes, our spouses legitimately aren't behaving in a way that they should be. Sometimes, they are just immature and we have to pray for God to grow them. Other times, we end up placing unrealistic expectations on our spouse and they fall short because they can't be God for us.

Our spouses cannot be everything for us all the time. They cannot make us feel happy all the time and they shouldn't be required to. A lot of dissatisfaction in marriage comes from us expecting too much from our marriage or our spouse when we should be looking toward God for that fulfillment.

If your relationship with God is right, you will not put demands on your spouse and your marriage to compensate for your spiritual emptiness.

I (Gloria) used to look to Robert to encourage me every time I got depressed. I would get angry and upset when he couldn't lift me out of my depression. I made him feel like a failure when he couldn't give me the joy, peace and hope that I should've been getting from God. But he wasn't the failure. I was looking in the wrong place for fulfillment.

God gives us a spouse to help us and encourage us through life and he gives us to our spouse to help them and encourage them. But our spouses cannot give us the fullness of life that only God can provide.

Focusing on your relationship with God – loving and being obedient to Him will end up freeing you to more deeply love and respect your spouse. God can use marriage to move us closer to Him and with that closeness comes a joyfulness in marriage that can truly surpass any spousal imperfections.

FOCUS ON THE GOOD STUFF

Appreciation goes a long way – in business, with friends, in your relationship with God and your relationship with your spouse. If we can get to the place where we can truly love and accept our spouse just as they are and yet be willing to make adjustments on ourselves to make our marriages better, then we're halfway there. The other half of the equation is for us to learn how to appreciate our spouses and make them aware that we appreciate them.

Dwell on their Good Qualities

There is ALWAYS something you can appreciate about your spouse, choose to constantly think and talk about those things.

> *"Finally, brothers and sisters, whatever is true, whatever is noble, whatever is right, whatever is pure, whatever is lovely, whatever is admirable – if anything is excellent or praiseworthy – think about such things."*
> *-Philippians 4:8 (NIV)*

We love how Philippians seems to emphasize that "if ANYTHING is excellent or praiseworthy…" It's as if the author (Paul) is acknowledging that there is an extensive list of legitimate negatives and complaints, but if there is even one thing that could be good, in any way, to dwell on that one thing.

Applying this to your marriage is hopefully not as extreme of a scenario. After all, at some point in your life, if not currently, you were head over heels in love with your spouse and wanted to spend every minute of every day with them for the rest of your life. So there had to be at least one thing about them that you truly liked. Perhaps over time, the blindingly good qualities lost their freshness and you started to see all the flaws in your spouse.

I (Gloria) have always credited myself with being a "brutally honest" person. For whatever reason, I used to always associate honesty with negativity. If someone asked me for my "honest" opinion, something in my brain told me that they were looking for a negative critique. And although they were usually asking for me to point out the flaws, that doesn't mean that I couldn't also point out all the good things. And it most certainly didn't mean that I had to walk away with only the negatives imprinted in my mind.

Acknowledging flaws in your spouse doesn't mean that you have to dismiss all their good qualities and dwell only on the negative. And focusing on the good stuff doesn't mean that you throw up blinders and live in denial of areas where your spouse needs improvement. We're suggesting that you can acknowledge that your spouse has flaws, help when you can but then walk away with their good traits at the forefront of your mind. Choose to only think about and talk about the good things in your spouse.

The cultural tendency is to define reality by whatever is the most negative. But just because you choose to focus on the positive elements of a situation or person doesn't mean you are living in denial. In fact, people who choose to only see what's negative in a situation are living in just as much denial as those who refuse to admit there is anything negative at all. Both positive and negative elements exist in almost any scenario or person, so why not choose to believe the best?

For instance, we saw this wonderful meme warning the social media population of the dangers of a particular chemical compound that was found in nearly everything they consumed. The facts were listed as follows: it can be chemically synthesized by burning rocket fuel, over-consumption can cause excessive sweating, urination and even death, 100% of all serial killers, rapist and drug dealers have admitted to drinking it, it is the primary ingredient in herbicides and pesticides, it's the leading cause of drowning and finally, 100% of all people exposed to it will die. Sounds pretty horrific! Judging by the facts presented, it certainly makes you want to find out what it is so you can make sure you steer your family clear of this terrible chemical compound! Guessed what it is yet? Water.

Even though everything that was stated about water in the meme described is completely factual, only focusing on the negative facts made the most essential, life-giving chemical on our planet sound like a toxic disaster. So it is with everything in life, including our marriages.

If you choose to only talk about what's wrong with your spouse and what they need to work on and every time you think about your spouse, you get frustrated by their imperfections - what you once were blindly in love with can all of a sudden look like something you can no longer stand to have in your life. It's not living in denial to not focus on the negative - it's choosing to give your marriage life in your thinking instead of trying to destroy it.

Stop Complaining

So how do you give your marriage life? Stop complaining. Stop thinking or talking about all the things you don't like about your spouse or you wish they would change. It's really that simple.

> *"Watch the way you talk. Let nothing foul or dirty come out of your mouth. Say only what helps, each word a gift. Make a clean break with all cutting, backbiting, profane talk. Be gentle with one another, sensitive. Forgive one another as quickly and thoroughly as God in Christ forgave you."*
> *-Ephesians 4:29,31 (MSG)*

The more you complain, the more you are reaffirming and reminding yourself of all the bad things about your spouse – and the more you'll dislike them. It's a very logical process. If you sit around and constantly remind yourself how bad you have it, you are going to make yourself depressed. Sometimes all it takes is a change of perspective.

One night, I (Gloria) got pretty upset with him because I was feeling overwhelmed and I didn't feel like he was doing enough to help me fix things around the house. Never mind that he helped me watch the kids in the evenings, did the dishes a couple times that week, pulled out all the weeds in the yard without me asking and brought me the baby in the wee hours of the morning when I was too tired to get out of bed myself.

All I could think about was the drape that got pulled down and needed to be put back up, the kitchen chairs that needed to be fixed and the ottoman that had a broken leg. I'd been asking him to do those things for a week and even though he had time to sit down and watch 45-minutes of a TV show on two separate occasions that week, he neglected to spend at least one of those opportunities fixing something. So I got upset. Thinking back through things the next morning, I realized how immensely grateful I should've been to have a husband that helped me as much as he did.

It's amazing how trivial the negative things become when you put them in perspective alongside all the things you can be grateful for. For everything that you can complain about, you can also find just as many things to be grateful about.

Appreciate that they are Different

If your spouse was just like you, then they wouldn't need you to complete them and you wouldn't need them to balance you out. If you can think of nothing else to be grateful for, be grateful that there is something they need your help with.

For example, I (Robert) can be pretty forgetful about certain things. I remember one time I kept forgetting to take the trash out. Gloria reminded me when I woke up, put a post-it note eye-level on the door that I use to leave the house and then put the trash bag in the middle of my walking path in the garage. I moved it to the side in order to make multiple trips putting some things in my car, then by the time I actually got in my car, I forgot all about the trash bag. She would get frustrated at me for a while, but then she had an epiphany. If I weren't so forgetful, then she wouldn't have the unique opportunity to find ways to help me in my weakness. She appreciated that I appreciated that she was there to help me not forget.

There is a massive list of things that you can appreciate about your spouse depending on how you spin it. Appreciate that they always look so nice when they go out or appreciate that they are comfortable going out relaxed and aren't so concerned about having to put-on appearances. Appreciate that they eat dinner at the table with the family when they could be working or appreciate that they have mad video-gaming skills and know how to step away from work and take a break. If you put in a little effort into changing your perspective, you can find something good about each situation.

Before finishing this chapter, grab a pen and paper. Do you have it yet? No, ok. Got it yet? We'll wait...

Ok, now we want you to make a list of what you CAN appreciate about your spouse. Not just what you DO appreciate about them (although you can include them as well) but what you CAN (if you changed your perspective a little) appreciate about them. We're not going to assign a number to achieve. If you've only added one thing to your list, that's all you need, but chances are, if you take some time, you'll be able to fill out both sides of that sheet of paper.

METHODS OF APPRECIATION

Now that you've got a list of things you can appreciate about your spouse, these are some practical ways to communicate those things to your spouse. This is not an extensive list by any means, but hopefully it'll get you on the right track.

Tell Them

This one's pretty self-explanatory. No matter how seemingly insignificant, if you think of something you like about your spouse, immediately tell them. Call them, text them, post it on their wall, tag them in your story, send a carrier pigeon – get the message across to them however you can. The smallest statement of appreciation can mean the world to someone. Combine each small complimentary comment over the course of months and you could have a completely different marriage.

Robert tends to be forgetful, and says he thinks of good things to tell me but then forgets by the time he gets to a place that he can tell me. So we developed a work-around. Every night, or as often as we can, when we are winding down for the day, we tell each other three things that the other person did that day that we appreciated. It doesn't have to be anything big or extravagant. One night, Robert's three things for me were: 1- that he went to go find some baby powder from the bathroom closet and noticed how easy it was to find because everything was in its proper place and appreciated that I kept things organized, 2- he liked that I told our son a funny story before bedtime and finally 3- he liked the shirt I was wearing that day. Those are fairly small things and nothing that I do that's out of the ordinary from what I do any other day, but it was nice to hear that he noticed those things.

Tell Others

Brag on your spouse to your friends, your family, on social media - let the world know how great they are. This has many benefits. First, it makes your spouse feel good to know you think something good about them. Second, it makes them much more confident because you are affirming, in front of their peers, that they are a successful spouse (public recognition can go a long way). Third, it's a layer of safeguard for your marriage from a potential affair. You are clarifying that you have a spouse, you're perfectly happy with them and no outsiders are needed. And finally, it helps you feel blessed by being married to your spouse.

Just like complaining can make you depressed about your marriage. Verbalizing your spouse's good qualities, especially publicly, can help you change your own perspective of your spouse and remind you of how good you have it. In essence, you create the spouse that you want.

Don't let your tokens of private and public appreciation just be empty words. Be genuine about your compliments and statements. Just because you choose to announce the 1 good quality out of the 99 negative ones doesn't mean you are lying or just putting on appearances. It means that you are making a conscience decision to affirm that one good quality. This is the marriage that you committed to. You can't (or shouldn't) get a new spouse and you can't really change the one you have, so you might as well dwell on the good stuff.

Respect Them

It's not just about saying how much you appreciate them, but how you respect them. It doesn't do you much good to publicly compliment them and then completely ignore them and devalue them behind closed doors. You'll just end up negating your efforts. Focus on your spouse's value in private as well. Listen to their thoughts and opinions and make them feel that they are of value to you. If you truly respect someone, you don't shut them out or shut them up, you care about what they have to say and take their opinions and contributions seriously.

Assist Them

Not good with verbalizations? Then create less work for them to do. Without them asking, do a chore they would normally do, or help them unwind after a long day. Key phrase, "without them asking." If your spouse has to ask you to help, then it's not really showing appreciation, it's more like fulfilling a request out of obligation. Taking the initiative to serve them in some capacity communicates that you recognize what they have to accomplish and what they contribute to the family and that their time is just as valuable as your time.

Make sure they feel appreciated!

There are so many ways to show appreciation. How you choose to appreciate your spouse will vary greatly based on your relationship and your personalities. The key takeaway for this section is that your spouse feels appreciated. Communicate with them and find out what you can do to make them feel appreciated and then do that.

LITTLE THINGS EQUAL BIG CHANGE

Can you imagine the shift in your marriage if you applied the content from this one chapter? What if we stopped expecting our spouses to meet an unreachable standard of perfection we created for them, were willing to change and grow ourselves and made an effort to focus and communicate what we appreciate about our spouses? In even as little as a week, the atmosphere of most of our marriages would change dramatically.

INTIMATE APPAREL

#sex #romance

culture • Romance is for fairy tales and sex ends after marriage
counter-culture • Romance is a part of marriage and sex just keeps getting better

ten

INTIMATE APPAREL

It's often said that sex ends after marriage and that romance is dead. In fact, we once heard a joke about a scientific breakthrough proclaiming that doctors had identified a food that diminishes the human being's sex drive by up to 80% - wedding cake. Ok, so that's obviously not true but that doesn't negate the fact that couples tend to lose their sexual connection not too long after the honeymoon. But God intends for the contrary to happen in your marriage! The Song of Solomon depicts a marriage that is not only filled with a vibrant (and adventurous) sex life, but also a marriage that is brimming with the sweet scents of romance.

So, what happened? Somehow, culture got it mixed up. Look at how sex and romance are portrayed these days. Nearly every TV show and movie suggests that before marriage, romance is at its height and sex is just a normal part of a dating relationship (or non-dating relationship depending on who you talk to). Then if you watch the TV shows and movies with married couples, the message is clear: married couples don't get sex or romance.

It's such a sad phenomenon that the two most intimate gifts that God designed for married life are in abundance outside of marriage and are nearly extinct inside most marriages (or so the media portrays it as such).

We're going to change up the flow a bit on this topic and tackle some points based on the common misconceptions that surround sex and romance.

SEX MISCONCEPTION #1: SEX ENDS AFTER MARRIAGE

There is a proper order for sex and marriage. Unfortunately, because many couples experience sex prior to marriage, sex is no longer an enlightening and invigorating gift that comes from marriage, but a pastime that seems to disappear as life gets busy. But that's a topic for another book. You're already married, so let's pick up the topic from there.

Since God didn't intend for sex to even begin until a couple are married, that fact alone should clear up the misconception that sex ends after marriage. God expects you to have a vibrant sex life after marriage.

What's Healthy?

You could argue that your sex life is a good indicator of the health of your marriage. That seems like a funny statement to make – especially in the Christian world where sex is often seen as a superficial and even slightly negative act – even if it's done within the confines of marriage. But sex, as God intended, is not superficial or perverted. There's a legitimate and spiritual weight to sex. It's a non-verbal way of recognizing that no matter what happens, you and your spouse are in it together. It's a constant physical reconciling that represents a spiritual oneness and comes out of an emotional closeness. Hence, for the most part, if you have a healthy marriage, you typically have a healthy sex life.

How do we define a healthy sex life? Well that differs from couple to couple. For some couples, having sex every day is required for both parties to feel content with their sex life. For other couples, once a week or once a month is all that is needed. The key to "healthy" is that both the husband and the wife are making a conscious and proactive decision to have enough sex to be satisfying for the both of them – regardless of what the societal norm is.

Emotional Consequences

We know that typically it's the husbands that are on the desiring end of the sex spectrum and the wives on the refusing end – but in an effort not to assume that every marriage is the same, we'll do our best to not stereotype sexual desires to a specific gender.

Just like there are obvious physical consequences of having sex outside of marriage – most of which you have probably heard of in sex-ED, there are desirable emotional consequences to having sex in marriage. An individual who feels sexually desired by their spouse (i.e. their spouse is proactive in initiating sex), will also grow in confidence in other areas of their life.

Passion in sex is a very healthy thing. A sexually fulfilled and active wife radiates a certain energy. A man who is sexually satisfied with his wife exudes a sense of confidence. A husband or a wife that is sexually satisfied is freed to focus on the other important things in their life.

Let's not underestimate the vast effects of being sexually depleted. An individual who is sexually frustrated might walk around with that cloud of frustration over their head at work, in regard to their faith and around their friends. They're likely to become selfishly preoccupied and self-absorbed.

There's just something about being sexually fulfilled that gives you the energy and attitude to conquer the world. And there's something about feeling sexually desirable that gives you a confidence that overflows into other areas of your life.

Although this could go both ways for men and women, I (Robert) do feel that this is especially true for men and goes a step further. Gloria could do everything else in our marriage right – brag about me, support me, allow me to lead, surprise me with coffee at work every day, but if she wasn't having sex with me, I wouldn't feel loved by her. It's not just that I would feel sexually frustrated or that I would feel undesirable, but I wouldn't feel emotionally connected to her. Just like Gloria needs emotionally in-depth conversations with me to feel connected to me, I need the physical act of sex to feel emotionally connected to her.

What's acceptable?

When we talk about a passionate sex life, questions might start forming regarding what's acceptable. In the Christian culture, modesty in your wardrobe and speech is given a high regard, but in sex, modesty is not a word that relates well to passionate.

God is a God of passion and He intended and desires for the sex between a husband and his wife to be equally passionate. Sexual intimacy in the right context is a form of spiritual expression and praise towards God.

We said it earlier and we'll say it again, sex is not perverted. It's physical passion in its purest form. Our culture has caused sex and anything related to sex to be perverted and viewed as perverted by distorting it. There are so many perversions of sex, that in our culture, to deem sex as a holy act, seems inappropriate. But it is a holy act – if used in the context that God intended.

What's acceptable sex-wise? We tried to sum it up in one statement: any sexual activity that is exclusively done between a consenting husband and his consenting wife together that is not unbiblical or illegal is probably acceptable. We wouldn't make that the end-all statement in regard to what's appropriate in your sex life, but it's a good place to start.

Therefore, if you AND your spouse are interested in exploring some "creative" sexual acts or positions, if it's not clearly stated as biblically wrong, we say give it a shot. Have fun. Be creative. Yes, that sexual act you're thinking about right now (if not immoral, or unbiblical) is probably OK. However, be sure your motive for trying these new ideas is birthed out of your desire to explore greater sexual intimacy with your spouse and is not something you're trying to recreate out of a past relationship or porn addiction.

If motives in sex are wrong, it will feel cheap and devalued. It's not what you're doing that is cheap, but cheap is how you (or your spouse) will feel about it if it's motivated by something other than a sexual desire for more of them.

SEX MISCONCEPTION #2: SEX IS JUST PHYSICAL

Sex is not just physical. Sex always has spiritual and emotional implications. To treat or view sex as exclusively physical act is evidence of an emotional and spiritual depravation and if continued, only leads to further negative spiritual and emotional consequences.

Sex, used appropriately, is a gift that reaps many positive benefits including both physical enjoyment and emotional intimacy with your spouse. That doesn't mean that every time you have sex with your spouse it should only be a serious spiritual or intensely intimate experience.

Think of your non-sexual interactions with your spouse: Sometimes you may talk about deeply emotional vulnerabilities, sometimes you are playfully debating which restaurant has the best shrimp and grits, sometimes you are exploring new ideas for your future and sometimes you are just texting to let your spouse know not to forget to pick-up the kids at 5pm. Not every interaction you have with your spouse is a deeply intimate conversation, but all the interactions collectively connect you to your spouse in one way or another – even if that connection is just the logistics of living life together.

So it is with sex. Part of the gift of sex is all the different ways that it can take shape within your marriage and whether it's quick and spontaneous, slow and romantic, just handling business or anything in between, it's a representation of your commitment to each other. Sex is an outward expression of your inward commitment to your spouse and anything less is an insult to how God intended it to be.

The Eye of the Beholder

Even when we talk about physical attractiveness – it's not just physical. Sexual desirability is not universal – meaning, not everyone in the world finds the same physical features attractive. That seems like an obvious statement: some people prefer blondes or curves or chiseled abs - and the physical preferences continue.

But it becomes even more extreme when you look at it from a cultural perspective. In the US, a carved-out waistline with a flawless skin tone is usually considered desirable. However, in other parts of the world, the larger a woman, the more desirable – to the point that some girls are force-fed to increase their physical desirability – a practice referred to as "leblouh".[1] There are parts of the world where slight imperfections are considered more beautiful than flawless faces – crooked teeth (called "yaeba" in Japan[2]), facial moles, you name it – some culture in the world probably finds that trait sexually desirable.

The diversity in the cultural definition of beauty tells us that there is no tried and true universal standard of beautiful. Beauty – and sexual desirability – are a cultural phenomenon. And if it's learned culturally, that means it can be changed by an adjustment in an individual's perspective. Perspective is strongly controlled by emotion and the element of choice. So beauty is indeed in the eye of the beholder.

What does that mean for you specifically? It means that not only is sex not physical, but why or why you aren't sexually and physically attracted to your spouse, is also not just physical. If you ever think to yourself that you would desire your spouse more sexually if certain things about their physical appearance changed, you wouldn't be entirely correct. Predictably, like most other things in marriage, it's not so much about your spouse changing, it's more about you changing your perspective. In this case, you seeking God's assistance in changing your sexual attractions to align with what your spouse has to offer.

Does this mean that if your spouse changed their physical appearance to suit your preferences that you wouldn't find them more attractive? The simple answer is no. If you are arguing that your spouse could be more sexually attractive to you by changing their physical appearance, then you're probably making an accurate statement.

However, should your spouse HAVE to change their physical appearance for you to be more sexually attracted to them? Is that the only way for you to be more sexually attracted to them? Is that the right way to tackle the issue of a lack of sexual attraction? The answers to all of these things is what we're discussing here.

If you aren't feeling sexually attracted or aroused by anything about your spouse, then that's a different topic in a different book – maybe you should seek some medical help or change your diet up a bit. For this book, we are assuming that you are sexually attracted to something about your spouse. If you are having issues with finding your spouse sexually attractive, then something is going on with you – not necessarily your spouse or their physical attributes. Perhaps you're disconnected emotionally, perhaps you have visually trained yourself to find specific physical attributes attractive by what you see on a regular basis or maybe you have attached certain physical characteristics to a positive emotion through inappropriate relationships with people of the opposite sex other than your spouse.

Whatever your spouse looks like, you can make the choice to be more sexually attracted to them. That doesn't mean that it's wrong for you to want your spouse to dye their hair a certain color or lose some weight or bulk up so they are more sexually attractive to you – or for them to want to do those things for you. What it does mean, is that your spouse changing themselves physically should not be the determining factor as to whether or not you are sexually aroused by your spouse.

To be clear, this should absolutely never be initiated as a "if you would do this, I would be more attracted to you" conversation. If a conversation of what physical traits you find attractive comes up, you had better be sure those conversations are delivered with love, and complete acceptance regardless of if they work toward your ideas or not.

Again, beauty is in the eye of the beholder. The more you fall in love with your spouse emotionally, the more they'll be attractive to you physically. Your definition of beauty is defined by what you love.

I Give

"It's good for a man to have a wife, and for a woman to have a husband. Sexual drives are strong, but marriage is strong enough to contain them and provide for a balanced and fulfilling sexual life in a world of sexual disorder. The marriage bed must be a place of mutuality – the husband seeking to satisfy his wife, the wife seeking to satisfy her husband."
-I Corinthians 7:2-3 (MSG)

If you've been in the church circuit long enough, you may already know that if you want to talk about the erotic nature of love Biblically, you go to the Song of Solomon. In Song of Solomon, the word "love" is used several times, as expected. But what's really interesting is the original Hebrew word for "love" – "ahavah".

In Hebrew, this word is comprised of three characters. The two foundational characters, literally translated, are translated as "I give." It's the third Hebrew character that modifies the entire word to mean "love." So even in the most sexualized book of the Bible – where breaking down the text may reveal explicit sexual content beyond just intercourse – the primary word they use for "love" doesn't even mean an "erotic" love – it's a sacrificial love.

As a culture, we've diminished sex to simply be a means to gratify erotic impulses, but we were created to be more than wild animals satisfying fleshly desires. God created sex to be a method in which a husband and a wife can demonstrate their sacrificial love physically. Healthy sex represents the give and take relationship that should be reflected in a healthy marriage.

I Corinthians 7:3 (MSG) states that the "marriage bed must be a place of mutuality – the husband seeking to satisfy his wife, the wife seeking to satisfy her husband." If one of you is always taking and the other is always expected to give, you may be missing out on the fullness that a healthy sex life can provide in your non-sexual relationship as husband and wife.

Friends with Benefits

Researching further into the Hebrew translation of "love" we also learn that occasionally, the word "ahava" is also used to mean "friendship."

Is the Bible condoning a "friends with benefits" relationship status? Let's not get crazy here. What this can teach us is that a healthy and passionate sex life within a marriage is based on a foundation of friendship as much as it is based on sexual desire.

Ultimately, it all fits together hand-in-hand. Great sex comes from a great friendship with your spouse and a great friendship comes from a deep connection and a deep connection comes from a willingness to sacrifice yourself.

Sure, you could have fleeting sex that provides surface-level enjoyment, but then you're only scratching the surface of how great sex really can be - and who wants to feel like their missing out on great sex?

It's not just physical.

When It Is "Just Physical"

I Corinthians 7:2 (MSG) says that "sexual drives are strong, but marriage is strong enough to contain them and provide for a balanced and fulfilling sexual life in a world of sexual disorder." In other words, we live in a sex-crazed world, but one of the reasons God gave us marriage was so that we could have a great sex life without getting sucked into the consequences of sexual sin.

Sex is a way to keep your sexual desires focused exclusively on your spouse. Outside influences, such as porn, distort your focus and drives you away from your spouse mentally, emotionally and physically.

If marriage is God's way for you to have your sexual desires fulfilled without sin, then porn completely negates any good that God intended for you to get out of sex. We've already pushed the point that sex isn't just physical – but porn takes something that was meant to have immense depth and makes it a shallow, physical thing and strips away all the other vital elements of what makes your marriage healthy.

There are many amazing books addressing porn, like Stephen Arterburn's "Every Man's Battle", so we don't feel the need to repeat what has already been said. However, because porn is so rampant, we definitely want to touch on it briefly.

Porn

Porn. There's a word that probably conjured up a lot of different emotions. A few churches discuss it openly, but for most churches it is a deeply taboo subject. Yet it is a topic that has more than likely affected each of our lives in some way. Porn, in any amount, will harm, if not destroy your marriage. If not legally ending your marriage, then emotionally and spiritually ending it.

Porn, as with many other sins, starts small and grows into something destructive – therefore even a small amount of porn is destructive. The real danger of porn in comparison to other life-threatening habits like drugs, alcohol, etc., is that it's such a hidden thing and the consequences are also primarily unseen until it's too late.

Arguably, it may be better for someone to have a drug or alcohol addiction, because those are visible habits that can be physically removed from someone's life and if nothing else, at least the people close to a drug addict or alcoholic are aware that that person needs help. Porn is private and the memory of the images of porn are forever accessible. It has the ability to destroy a life from the inside out without anyone ever knowing what happened.

And don't think that porn only affects the viewer. If you are married, it affects your spouse on the most intimate level. Porn can make your spouse feel worthless and ashamed - even if they aren't the ones participating in it. Porn will cause you to become greatly unsatisfied with your spouse to the point of emotional and verbal abuse. You may not even be aware that you are doing it, but when you have access to something that provides you with a high that your spouse cannot match, there is no way else for your brain to process the comparison except to diminish your spouse as "not good enough." Instead of loving and cherishing your spouse, you can become the attacker – tearing down your spouse's sense of emotional and sexual security.

If you are not able to experience a sexual desire for your spouse and you are engaging in porn, you're shooting yourself in the foot. You are causing your own problems. Porn can greatly decrease or altogether eliminate your sexual desire for your spouse.

Porn-related issues may not always pertain to only one spouse watching it in private. Watching porn with your spouse is just as damaging. An argument that we have heard often is that mutual porn seems OK because they weren't lusting after the actors in the videos, but it aroused them both sexually so they had an active sex life.

Although we can understand this logic, it's still dangerous for a number of reasons. Neither of us has a history of drug-use, but we've heard that having sex while on Ecstasy is a remarkable experience. We've also been told that the downside was that having sex without Ecstasy was so bland that it wasn't even worth it – so after experiencing sex with Ecstasy, the only way for them to experience sex at all was to continue using the drug.

You can apply the same logic to becoming dependent on watching porn in order to have an active sex life with your spouse. If you use porn to "get in the mood" long enough; eventually, you may be unable to "get in the mood" without porn. So then, the married couple that only started watching porn to gain a healthy sex life are now BOTH dependent on it. On top of that, because porn was invited into their marriage, it became a permissible element in their lives and finds its way into the individuals' lifestyle apart from his or her spouse.

More important than how it negatively affects your marriage, is how it effects your relationship with God. It breaks God's heart to see one of

His children, who He has great plans for, fall into such a dark pattern of pornography. Porn, although private, will keep you from being able to fulfill all that God has planned for you. Pornography is sin and inviting porn into your home and viewing it (even as a couple) is simply entertaining yourselves on sin. God's desire is that you are entertaining yourselves on each other.

And it's not that God withdraws Himself from you if you choose to watch porn, it's that you slowly withdraw yourself from Him. If you are a born-again believer, then as much as you try to hide it or not admit it, there is an element of shame every time you watch or look at porn. This constant shame, if not brought before God, will cause a person to withdraw from God. Any worship or devotion will feel slightly less genuine and so your relationship with God slowly dwindles to a surface-level religion. And you can't ever dig deeper with God because of what you refuse to let go of.

SEX MISCONCEPTION #3: SEX IS JUST A TOOL

We've driven home the point that sex is not just physical – sex has a purpose, emotionally and spiritually. But that purpose is not to be used as a tool. Sex is not something that should be used for money or to bargain with or just to procreate. It's not something you keep in your toolbox and pull out when you need to get some work done.

Sex is not a Bargaining Chip

Sex is a gift that each spouse holds for the other to remind them how desired they are. Sex should be given freely to your spouse without limitations or ransom. You glorify God by cultivating a sexual desire for your spouse and by welcoming your spouse's sexual desire for you.

When you start bargaining with sex or withholding sex because you're mad, you're treading into dangerous territory.

"Marriage is not a place to 'stand up for your rights.' Marriage is a decision to serve the other, whether in bed or out. Abstaining from sex is permissible for a period of time if you both agree to it, and if it's for the purposes of prayer and fasting – but only for such times. Then come back together again. Satan has an ingenious way to tempting us when we least expect it. I'm not, understand, commanding these periods of abstinence – only providing my best counsel if you should choose them." –I Corinthians 7:4-6 (MSG)

We're not going to come right out and say that refusing to have sex with your spouse is a sin, but the phrase "– but only for such times" certainly lends itself to the conclusion that it is not entirely permissible to abstain from sex when both you and your spouse do not agree or when the reason isn't for fasting or prayer.

We have to look at this scripture in context. In the New King James Version, this verse begins with the statement, "The wife does not have authority over her own body, but the husband does. And like-wise the husband does not have authority over his own body, but the wife does." Which tells us that the author was directly addressing the issue of husbands and/or wives who have the attitude that "this is my body and if I don't feel like having sex with you, I don't have to."

Obviously, there are plenty of logistical reasons why abstaining from sex may be unavoidable: military leave, severe illness or disablement, tragedy, and the list goes on. But this verse isn't addressing the logistical obstacles – it's addressing the obstacles related to how you as an individual within your marriage perceive the authority you have over your own body. Put simply, it's addressing our hearts.

When you got married, you became "one flesh", which means you no longer own your own flesh, your spouse owns your flesh and you no longer own only your flesh, you now own your spouse's flesh too. That means that you don't technically have the right to withhold yourself from yourself.

Let's look at this from a biological perspective. If a woman is pregnant, there are technically two lives in one body. Because the forming baby is the physically weaker being of the two people, the woman's body will

191

always make sure that the baby is cared for over the health of the woman. For instance, if the woman isn't drinking enough water or taking in enough nutrients, the woman's body will automatically take the water and nutrients that are available from the woman's body and pour it into the baby's body. The woman doesn't have a choice in the matter. She can't decide that she needs the water and nutrients and the baby will have to wait until later. Her body makes the decision for her automatically because there are two bodies in one and resources have to go where they are needed the most. Life-sustaining resources don't go where mom or baby "feel" like they should go.

The same type of "one flesh" relationship takes place in a marriage. You and your spouse are one flesh – ideally, each providing the other with what they need to survive in every aspect of their being. You cannot simply decide where resources (in this case, the resource is sex) need to go based on how you feel. If you or your spouse "need" sex; by default, it should be automatic for the spouse to provide it.

We're not saying that it has to operate that automatically in every situation, but the ultimate goal is that we understand it is God's will for us to meet the sexual needs of our spouse.

With that said, the strategy you put in place is something you and your spouse have to work out amongst yourselves. You could implement a 24-hour rule (where you can cancel but you must reschedule – and keep that appointment within 24 hours). If there is a time or energy constraint, perhaps you include alternative options for providing a sexual release for your spouse outside of long-lasting intercourse. We'll leave those options up to your imagination but there are ways to meet his or her need that do not include a marathon sex session. Maybe you should schedule it on the calendar to ensure no one "forgets". Although this may seem boring, another perspective is that it can bring excitement and anticipation for the event scheduled for the day. It's important to work something out with your spouse that you both can agree on that will leave each spouse sexually fulfilled within the marriage.

It ends up being a balancing act - husbands should sacrifice for their wives and wives shouldn't deny their husbands of sex "just because". If both people are making an effort to be generous to the other, you'll both meet somewhere in the middle.

The point we really want to drive home is this: as the norm, sex is to be given freely to your spouse without negotiations, guilt trips or threats. It should not be withheld as a form of punishment or a bargaining chip. Sex is not the wife's opportunity to manipulate the chain of command. Sex is not a business negotiation. In its purest form, it's a gift given to those that make the commitment of marriage.

As a disclaimer, in the off-chance someone wants to take these statements out of context and twist them to their own sinful justifications, we should also briefly mention that sex shouldn't be taken forcefully. Although your spouse's body may not be "their own", it is not in God's character to ever force His will onto someone else. God is our creator and we are all owned by Him and if He so desired, could be controlled by Him without a justifiable argument; but even so, God waits patiently for us to accept Him. Thus, this is the same attitude we should exhibit in every aspect of our marriages (and life).

On the opposite-side of the argument, remember that your spouse's body might not be their own, but yours is not your own either. This system setup by God is designed to push you and your spouse to a healthy agreement working together to meet each other's needs.

Sex is just for Procreation
We've made it abundantly clear that we do not have the right to utilize sex as an emotional tool within our marriage. We believe there are three Biblical reasons that sex was created: to physically symbolize the becoming of "one flesh" in a marriage, for pleasure and for procreation. What that means, is that you aren't any more religious or spiritual if you only have sex for procreation.

The idea of sex being used for pleasure is not something that our modern-day, western-civilization concocted in our minds. Yes, our culture certainly has perverted many aspects of sex, but the idea of sex being pleasurable is not in itself perverted. Sex between husband and wife feels good and is holy at the same time.

In the Jewish culture, the ability to preserve the family-line is of the utmost importance – after all, they are the "chosen people", so facilitating the existence of the "chosen people" is one of the most important aspects of their lives. But even in that culture, a Jewish woman had three rights: food, clothing and the "onah." "Onah" meaning the right to have sexual intercourse apart from the duty of procreation.[3]

Biology Lesson

It's simple to prove this "sex for pleasure" approach as God created parts of our anatomy to have no other purpose except for sexual pleasure. We can go down the list of almost every sexual organ and write out it's procreation-related purpose, but there are parts of our body that have absolutely no use except to provide a sensation of pleasure[4] – meaning that God intended for us to experience pleasure through sex.

Before we are married, we are bombarded with all the "bad" health risks of sex. But there are also some pretty impressive health benefits to sexual activity. These benefits were discovered by several different scientific studies over the past several years[5]. We clumped all the medical benefits into one big list, but these different positive side-effects are derived from different aspects of sexual activity.

The health benefits of sex, sexual activity and other components of sex include: acts as a natural anti-depressant, natural anxiety reducer, improves quality of sleep, increases energy, improves concentration, improves memory, improves mental alertness, assists with pregnancy maintenance, improves blood pressure, boosts immunity, increases self-esteem, increases female-initiated sexual behavior (the more a female has unprotected sex, the more chemicals are in her blood-stream that increase her libido), reduces pain ("I have a headache" can no longer be used as an effective excuse), dramatically reduces chances of prostate cancer, fights aging, heals internal and external wounds, boosts cardio health and according to a study done by North Carolina State University, it reduces the risk of breast cancer by 40%.

So, if you find yourself to be a depressed, grumpy, generally unhealthy person with absolutely no desire for sex and no energy; instead of medications, perhaps you should look into having more healthy, unprotected sex with your spouse. Major side note: depending on your family situation (your desire for kids or for more kids), you may need to find a way to schedule the "unprotected" requirement of most of these health benefits.

Holy Sex

The writings of Jewish culture even go a step further and explain that when a man and his wife engage in sex they are inviting the presence of God[6]. Sex is a huge part of a married individual's life. It's not just physical, it's not something you can use to throw your weight around (pun intended), it's not just so you populate the Earth and it most certainly should be a regular and active part of every marriage. Put aside the perversions and distortions of sex and realize that sex is a beautiful thing that was created by God as a gift to be experienced by married couples.

Every time we engage in pure-hearted sexual activity with our spouses, we are, in essence, glorifying God for His goodness and genius in His creation of sex.

ROMANCE

OK. Enough about sex already, let's talk about romance! When we think about romance, we tend to think about that guy who sweeps that girl off her feet and rides off into the sunset. Then the end credits roll.

If you build your entire marriage on the fairy-tale idea of romance, you'll end up being disappointed. Because there's a significant difference between the butterflies you feel when you "fall in love" and the foundational components that make-up a thriving marriage that leads to a true "happily ever after". We dive more deeply into that concept in Chapter 11: Lust vs. Love.

Romance in marriage should be more like the emotional dessert of a healthy relationship and less like the main course. Romance happens in moments and it can satisfy you for that moment, but it won't sustain you until the next time. It would be the equivalent of trying to live a healthy lifestyle by eating nothing but decadent desserts. If that's the only thing you ate, you may not live long enough to enjoy the next dessert or you'd be miserable in your life because your body wouldn't function as designed. Instead, a healthy and balanced lifestyle should consist of a healthy diet and the occasional dessert. In that way, you feel great living your life and can live long enough to experience your next dessert.

We assume everyone wants their marriage to last long enough to continue experiencing romance in their relationship. If that's the case, then your marriage has to be built on Biblical foundations found throughout this book and not just on the fleeting emotions that compose romantic moments.

DEFINING ROMANCE

What would you consider romantic? Rose petals leading to a candlelit dinner for two? Poetic nothings being whispered into your ear? A hand-made "I love you" sign being displayed on a jumbo screen at a football game? Your favorite flowers delivered to your office?

We all have our unique personalities and with that will come our own definitions of what we find to be romantic. But at the heart of every romantic act is one defining trait – it makes us feel special. We define something as romantic because it shows us that our spouse is paying exclusive attention to us or giving something to only us – which makes us feel special in some way.

The Knight in Shining Armor

To illustrate this point, let's look at a few different versions of a classic romantic scenario:

A knight in shining armor rides in on a beautiful white horse and defeats the dragon in order to save his princess. Romantic? Aside from the knee-jerk reaction for females to claim their independence and make sure everyone knows that they aren't a damsel in distress, most women would agree that at its core, it's a romantic ideal.

What if we changed the story up a bit? Now, a knight in shining armor rides in on a beautiful white horse and defeats the dragon in order to save an entire village of people – including his princess. Still romantic?

How about this version of the story: a knight in shining armor rides in on a beautiful white horse and defeats the dragon in order to save his princess? Then the next day, he rides into a different town to defeat another dragon to save someone else's princess because he's a good guy. Then the day after that, he goes into a third town and defeats another dragon to save an old man. Still romantic? The guy is obviously pretty successful in slaying dragons and he sounds like an upstanding citizen, but still romantic? Not so much.

Why did those little changes diminish the "romance"? After all, he saved his princess in every situation and he seems like a great guy. Alas, the alternate versions of the story seem significantly less romantic. Whether or not the act is romantic isn't about the knight saving his princess nor does it have anything to do with the princess being in distress and needing saving and it has nothing to do with how great the guy is. What made the story romantic is that the princess was so special to the knight that he risked his life just to save her.

If he saved a village as his knightly duty, it's a very courageous thing, but it doesn't really make her feel special – he's just doing a great job. In the third version of the story, every time he does the exact same thing for other people, it diminishes the romance for his princess. Why? Because it was romantic because she was special and the more the same act is repeated for other people, the less special it becomes and hence, the less romantic it becomes.

In order for something to be special, Google says it has to be better, greater, or otherwise different from what is usual. What makes something romantic is not necessarily a romantic act. It's that whatever the act is, makes the person on the receiving-end feel like they are more important or special in some way than anyone else.

Romance has no Comparison

> *"Let your fountain be blessed and rejoice in the wife of your youth. As a*
> *loving hind and a graceful doe, let her breasts satisfy you at all times;*
> *be exhilarated always with her love."*
> *-Proverbs 5:18-19 (NASB)*

These days, we laugh at a scripture like Proverbs 5:18-19. It seems a little bizarre to us. But if we look at the subtext of this scripture, we'll see a glimpse of the romance that God intended us to have in our marriages.

First, the scripture is not saying to like breasts in general. For a guy, we're pretty sure that's almost always a given. The verse clarifies whose breasts the husband should be satisfied with, "the wife of his youth."

That statement tells us two things: one, it's HIS wife's breasts he should be enamored with and two, those breasts aren't young anymore. For those of you who are just starting out on this journey of life, it may be a shock for you to learn that after childbirth and several years pass by, a woman's breasts and her body tend to change. The same is true for men. Without medical intervention, you simply don't have the same body at 60-years-old as you did when you were 20-something. Yet, if sex and romance is done God's way, you don't need plastic surgery for your spouse to continue to satisfy you even in their old age.

Proverbs is instructing a husband to be so in love and so enthralled by his own wife that it doesn't matter what breasts every other woman has and it doesn't matter what his wife's breasts look like in their older or post-childbirth years.

The husband in Proverbs is not just settling for his wife. He's so in love with her, he's exhilarated by her love. That's a big word. Other translations use the word "intoxicated" with her love.[7] His love for her is the same in his old age as it was when their love (and bodies) were young.

In fact, their love is much greater. When they were young, they had their youthful bodies to keep each other enticed and complement their emotional feelings. But in their old age, the husband's love transcends all superficial forms of attraction.

I (Gloria) am not sure that men can relate to the level of romance in the verse and what it is describing, but I think most women can. For me, there is nothing more romantic than for Robert to be so blinded by his love for me that he melts away all my most private insecurities despite my constant comparisons to my old self or to other women.

In simpler terms, the wife in Proverbs 5:19 is special to the husband. She is unlike anyone else in his life. To him, she is better, she is greater, and there is no competition.

ROMANCE MISCONCEPTIONS #1: ROMANCE COSTS MONEY

Romance is not about how much money you spend or what elaborate gesture you plan. It's about your heart and how you are able to express how special your spouse is to you.

If the only requirement in being romantic is that you find some way to make your spouse feel special, that opens up a slew of inexpensive options.

It also gives you a good starting point for the anti-girly girl. Your wife doesn't fit the mold of the damsel in distress? Fine, neither do I (Gloria). But that doesn't relieve you of the task of finding ways to make her feel special.

Special doesn't have to cost a lot of money - but it does have to cost something. It can cost time, attention, effort, emotional energy. The key here is that it has to be a gesture out of the ordinary to make your spouse feel special and if you are doing something you always do or always should do, that doesn't qualify as special.

You can take the time to write your spouse a note telling them how much you love them. You can stop by an ice cream shop on the way home and pick up their favorite ice cream. You can call them out of the blue and tell them you were thinking of them. You can quietly become vulnerable and share your emotions with your spouse. You can spontaneously post a status update on social media declaring your love for them when it's NOT their birthday, Mother's Day, anniversary, etc. (remember – special, what wouldn't be normal or expected).

One of my (Gloria) personal favorites is when I heard from someone else all the wonderful things that Robert said about me to his co-workers. It made me feel special for many reasons: that he thought of me when he wasn't around me, that he thought so highly about me, that it was obvious he wasn't expecting anything in return (because I wasn't even there and he didn't know I would find out about it) and he publicly declared it. It didn't cost him a penny, but it made me cry (which, to be fair, isn't difficult to do, but romantic nonetheless).

ROMANCE MISCONCEPTIONS #2: ROMANCE IS JUST TO GET SEX

This leads us to our next misconception about romance. Romance might get them in the mood, but if you do something for the purpose of getting them in the mood, it's no longer considered romance - just deception.

The whole point of something being romantic is demonstrating that someone is special to you and if you are only doing something special for your spouse because you want something in return, then that doesn't make them feel special. It makes them feel manipulated.

On top of it not being romantic, it attacks a female's most basic need of feeling secure in your relationship. If the only time that you ever tell your spouse how special they are to you is when you want something, then how are they ever supposed to truly know how you feel? There's no surety in that. No security.

ROMANCE MISCONCEPTIONS #3: SEX IS ROMANTIC

There may be a select few out there that determine that wanting to have sex with your spouse qualifies as making them feel special and therefore qualifies as romantic. Although, in some situations, having sex may qualify as a romantic gesture, we feel that in most cases, it simply doesn't qualify.

For one, the physical act of sex can happen between any male and any female. We are not saying that it should happen between any two random people, but we all understand that biologically, it can happen between any two random people. Hence, it doesn't make your spouse feel special if you want to have sex with them because it doesn't clearly communicate that you want to have sex with only them. Simply wanting to have sex with your spouse only communicates that you want sex and they are your only moral option.

Romance requires that you don't make your spouse feel like they are the only option; but rather, that if you were given all the options in the world, your spouse is the only one you would ever choose or want to be with. This is difficult to communicate through a desire for sex on its own.

In fact, if the only time you ever show your spouse that you want them and they are special is when you approach them for sex, this can end up making your spouse feel common and like nothing more than a glorified prostitute. Instead of feeling special, your spouse can end up feeling used.

As we mature, most people realize that someone wanting to have sex with you does not make you special because it's not YOU they want, it's the sex. In the context of marriage, this can quickly develop a jealousy of sex in your marriage. If sex seems to be getting all the husband's attention and all the husband's desire, the wife can end up feeling like the "middle-man" in the marriage between her husband and sex. This doesn't make the wife feel special. If sex were a person, this would make sex feel special.

Your spouse has to know that they are the most amazing person in your life – not just because of something they can provide for you, but because they are that special to you. Being able to communicate that - that's romantic.

SEX & ROMANCE MISCONCEPTIONS #4: DOING SOMETHING ROMANTIC IS THE SAME THING AS BEING ROMANTIC

Ever hear the statement, "if I have to ask, then it doesn't count"?

We've discussed in earlier chapters that men and women do not think alike and that we have to learn to communicate exactly what we want instead of hoping our spouses will read our minds.

However, when it comes to romance, it's not so much that your spouse wants you to figure out how to express your love to them as much as it is that in order for something to be truly romantic, it requires the desire to do it. If you are only doing exactly what your spouse asked of you, then it feels more like obedience than romance.

As far as romance is concerned, your spouse doesn't want you to just go through the motions. If they want romance, they want you to be so in love with them that it's just spilling out of you and if you don't express it somehow, you'll explode. Ok, maybe that's a bit of an exaggeration, but it's along those lines.

Simply doing a romantic gesture without your heart invested in order to be "romantic" is the equivalent to your spouse just having sex with you but thinking about how much laundry they have to do. At the end of the day, both technically got an act of romance and an act of sex, but it's nothing compared to a romantic gesture that stems from a heart that truly thinks their spouse is amazing or sex that is initiated with passion.

BACK TO BASICS

Most husbands want their wives to desire them sexually because of what he can do for her, and not just for who he is. Wives want their husbands to desire them romantically for who she is, not just for what she can do for him. It goes back to the basic core needs of respect and security. Husbands like to be respected and feel successful and wives want to feel secure in their husband's love for them. Sex and romance are relational ways to further support those needs.

The next time you have sex with your spouse or do something romantic for them, before you proceed, take a moment to focus on why you are doing what you are doing. Taking just a little effort to actually get in the mood before sex or meditating on the amazingness of your spouse before you do something romantic, will eventually develop into the norm in your marriage and over time your marriage will be overflowing with satisfying sex and romance.

WHAT'S LOVE GOT TO DO WITH IT?

#lust #love

culture • Follow your heart
counter-culture • Follow God's Word and your heart will follow

eleven

WHAT'S LOVE GOT TO DO WTIH IT?

We are a society driven by our emotions. Our culture determines what the "right" decision is based on how we feel instead of what God states to be true in His Word. We tend to live for the next emotional high – whether in a movie, someone else's life or our own lives. The dependence many of us have on our emotions to make us feel "alive" has sadly left behind a trail of broken homes and broken people in its wake.

It is not God's intention for us to have a passionless marriage or a lifeless existence. Our emotions are a gift from God to give our lives color, but we must learn to control them and give them boundaries so they are used to create a masterpiece instead of a splattered mess.

DEFINING OURSELVES

There's a bigger difference between "lust" and "love" than most people realize. But before we can dive into the differences, we have to have a clear understanding of who we are and how we relate to other people.

Matthew 28:19 NKJV tells us that God is made up of three parts, "the Father and the Son and of the Holy Spirit." We also know that "God created man in His own image…" (Genesis 1:27 NKJV). Hence, we understand that we also consist of three parts: our "whole spirit, soul, and body…" (I Thessalonians 5:23 NKJV).

As beings that contain all of these components - components that are often at war with themselves, we are complicated creatures indeed. It becomes even more complicated when we begin to analyze how these three parts of our existence interact with each other and how they are influenced by outside stimuli and other equally complicated beings.

The Dog Metaphor

It may be easier to visualize who we are if you think of yourself as a person walking a dog on a leash: your physical body is the dog, your soul is the leash and your spirit is the dog-walker.

As you take your dog (body) for a walk in the world, the dog is confronted with many stimuli. It's natural for your dog to get a whiff of something in the air and take notice, see a squirrel and want to immediately go chase it or smell another dog and innately become aggressive if it's the same sex or be uncontrollably attracted if it's a dog of the opposite sex. But no matter the stimuli or distraction, if the dog is on a leash and the dog-walker is in firm control, it doesn't take much to yank the dog back on the right path and refocused on where he should be going. The dog-walker is in control and what it produces is a beautiful and peaceful walk through the park with both dog-walker and dog arriving at the appointed destination.

That's the ideal scenario. Unfortunately, what is far more common to see in our world, metaphorically speaking, is a big dog running rampant in the streets attached to a leash that is dragging behind it either a dead dog-walker (non-Christian) or a terribly weak and feeble dog-walker (weak Christian) that is helplessly stumbling after the dog. This creates a situation where we have a dog that is wreaking havoc on the streets chasing down every whiff in the air, overreacting in fear to every trash can clanking together and/or relieving itself in the middle of sidewalks for others to accidentally step in. A loose, out-of-control dog is bad enough, but this dog is also dragging a leash and a person on the other end, which multiplies the wreckage exponentially.

This is what our life is like when our body - our flesh - is in total control and our spirits are too weak to mandate otherwise. Every decision we make is based on our biological response, our soul (mind, will and emotions) quickly aligns itself with our bodies as it's dragged through the mud and our spirits – the only part of us that has any spiritual sense – is helplessly dragged behind.

Remember, that in our example, the dog, the leash and the dog-walker are permanently attached to each other – just as our body, soul and spirit have no choice but to coexist until our body dies. So simply letting go of the leash is not a viable option – the only way for the dog-walker (our spirit) to gain control of the dog (our bodies) is to become stronger than the dog. The leash, representing our soul, will always fall into alignment with and support whichever party is in control – whether that means we are dragging our souls through the mud or our souls are being kept clean and being used for a purpose.

This is a prime visual for the statement, "strengthening your spirit and starving your flesh" in relation to becoming a more mature believer. That advice is spot-on, but many times it's difficult for people to grasp and apply appropriately to their lives.

If you are living a life where "you present your bodies a living sacrifice, holy, acceptable to God" (Romans 12:1 NKJV), then metaphorically speaking, you are a 250lb bodybuilder walking a 5lb toy poodle. It doesn't matter how distracted that toy poodle may get or how much it may have the urge to chase after something, you, as the bodybuilder would not have any issues keeping your toy poodle in line. That doesn't mean that the toy poodle doesn't get urges - it does, but it is on a leash that is being controlled by a bodybuilder; therefore, everything is in alignment.

So then, how do we turn our "250lb Saint Bernard dragging behind a starved, half-dead, 80lb person on life support" scenario into the "5lb toy poodle being walked by a 250lb bodybuilder" scenario? How do we strengthen our spirits and weaken our flesh?

Spend a few minutes taking an inventory of the things that feed your flesh, then begin the process of starving your flesh of those things. If something catches our attention, don't let your eyes linger. If a pastime always leads to being overpowered with temptation, drop the pastime. If a thought enters your head, don't dwell on it – shift what you are thinking about. Find some accountability with this to help with the journey.

At first, it starts with small morsels of starvation – the little "wins". Even when you don't feel like a small decision matters, every opportunity that you have to deny your flesh of what you know is not in alignment with God's Word, you are slowly starving your flesh. This is one of the reasons that fasting is so incredibly powerful. It's an opportunity to go above and beyond our normal "right" decisions and completely deplete our flesh of its life source – food. If your flesh is already weak, then fasting is a way to make sure it's good and dead. If your flesh needs to be weakened, then fasting will give you a really strong start on your journey. If fasting is a new concept for you, then we highly recommend the book "Fasting" by Jentezen Franklin.[1]

However, it doesn't do you much good to have a weak flesh and still have a weak spirit. Metaphorically, then you're a 5lb toy poodle being walked by a 20lb 1-year-old just learning to walk. When the toy poodle gets the urge to chase after something, it's going to be a struggle to get the poodle back into alignment – sometimes the poodle will win and sometimes the 1-year-old will win.

It's equally important to do things to strengthen our spirits – through prayer, reading our Bibles, fasting and worship – things that draw us closer to our spirit's life source – God. Another important but less popular discipline is obedience. Every opportunity for obedience to God and His Word is an invitation into intimacy. It's you making a choice to deny the flesh for the sake of Christ. Even the small acts of obedience are rewarded by the strengthening of your Spirit. It may be a struggle to engage in those spiritual disciplines at first (because remember, your mind, will and emotions are easily swayed to support whichever part of you is stronger) and it may seem like nothing comes out of it, but keep going and slowly your spirit will grow and become a 250lb bodybuilder.

Jesus tells us in Matthew 26:14 to "keep watching and praying that you may not enter into temptation; the spirit is willing, but the flesh is weak" (NASB). Essentially what Jesus is telling us is that our Spirit is always in agreement with the will of God and our flesh is always in opposition and the only way to bring them into alignment is through prayer which is drawing us into a deeper and more intimate relationship with God by strengthening our spirit making it possible to bring our flesh into submission. The greatest experience will be when your soul makes the transition from being dragged in the mud behind your body and is finally lifted up into the air and supports the direction of your spirit – that moment when you experience the emotional desire to draw closer to God and crave His presence, instead of always having to force yourself to do it.

Perhaps having to grow your spirit and weaken your flesh seems like a lot of work and you are saying to yourself, "I just want to live free and happy…I want to be the dog living in the wild, free to do my own thing." The problem is, that doesn't exist. Sure, if you are a dog without a leash or perhaps just a short leash, then perhaps you could run wild and be happy. But you're not just the dog. You're also the leash and the walker. You're a three-fold being. So even if you are allowed to chase after every rabbit "freely", you may find some fleeting happiness in the moment, but you're still attached to the dead person on the other end and that dead person will always be the dead-weight that brings you down after you've caught all the wild rabbits that your little heart desires.

Ask almost any dog expert and they'll tell you, the happiest dogs are not the strays living in the streets, nor are they the dogs that are spoiled, but still unloved. The happiest dogs are the ones that are trained for a purpose and loved and valued by their owners.[2] When we have a genuine relationship with a loving God who trains us and leads us into the purpose we are created for – that's when we are truly "happy".

So "free and happy" is an oxymoron. It should be "unleashed and empty" or "submitted and happy" because there is no "free and happy".

How we Relate to Others

Having established the elements that make up who we are internally, we can now shift to how we relate to others. Similarly to the parts that make up our being (body, soul, spirit), there are three ways we can relate to others around us.

We can respond biologically (body) - any response that can be detected in a measurable, physical sense. We can relate to someone mentally or metaphysically through our mind, will and emotions (soul) – for instance, when we "like" someone, have a "connection" or feel an emotion towards someone or something. Finally, we can relate to people on a spiritual level (spirit) – when we care about someone's well-being or love them.

You can feel any one of those components towards a person. Two out of three of the components makes someone a valuable person in your life and all three components is what you should have with your spouse in order to have a truly fulfilled marriage.

LUST

Defining the difference between "lust" and "love" can be a daunting task, especially when Google defines "lust" as a "very strong sexual desire" and it defines "love" as an "intense feeling of deep affection." Biblically, both of those definitions would actually fall under the word "lust" and "love" would remain largely undefined by our world. If a well-meaning couple were to attempt to build their marriage on "love" according to Google's definition, they may find themselves questioning their "love" for their spouse when they no longer "felt" anything. A simple mis-definition of words can cause our entire worlds to crumble. This mis-definition goes even further when we look at how the Bible defines "love" in the next section.

Culturally, "lust" is usually understood to be a desire that's sexually-driven, to the point of perversion. Some people may more accurately define "lust" as a strong desire for anything that satisfies our bodies (sex, food, drink, material goods, etc.). Biblically, the word used for "lust" is "'avah" – literally meaning "to desire, crave (as in for food or drink)" or "to desire, long for, lust after (of bodily appetites)".[3] The word "lust" is used in scripture to describe something sinful or righteous depending on the context of the verse. Given the wide-array of definitions for "lust" in our culture, for the intents and purposes of this chapter, we'd like to define "lust" as a romantic attraction to someone that is so intense that you can feel it physically.

When we first meet someone, our first judgements are usually biological. Are they physically attractive to us? Did they "take our breathe away" when we first saw them? Or were we repelled by their appearance? These things are biological responses that can be further heightened by our growing mental response to someone.

The more we get to know a person, we begin to determine whether we have a mental connection with them. Do we like them or not? Do we have similar interests? Do we like hanging out with them or do they drive us crazy? The deeper we dive into a mental connection with someone, the more we use words like "soul connection", "kindred spirits" and finally "soulmates" to describe the intensity of the mental connection we have.

As our "souls connect", so do the biological responses to that person – cue the butterflies, dilated pupils and sweaty palms. The problem is, it's at this point that our culture defines "love" and that's where the confusion lies and wreaks havoc on our lives.

These biological responses fall under the "lust" category. Yes, the mental connection may be entirely legitimate, but the biological responses that exist during this phase are all being misattributed to "love", when in fact, real "love" has nothing to do with emotions at all.

Like we said earlier, you need all three connections with your spouse to have a fulfilling marriage – the biological connection, mental connection and spiritual connection. However, to attribute such temporal biological reactions to "love" is insulting to who God is – if "God is Love" (I John 4:8 NKJV) and God "do[es] not change" (Malachi 3:6 NKJV), then "love" can most certainly not be defined by emotions and biological responses that have proven themselves to be so circumstantially temporal.

Lust is not necessarily wrong in all contexts. It's a vital part of how God created us and is an essential phase for how we develop a relationship with our spouse in the first place. But if lust develops with someone who is not your spouse or if lust is the sole vehicle that drives the connection between you and your spouse, that's a problem.

The Downfalls

When I (Gloria) think of the first time I had that feeling for Robert, I think of two brilliantly orchestrated moments. Now, we were high school sweethearts, so you'll have to put on your teenage-drama hat for these to make any kind of sense. The first time I felt a physical attraction to Robert was when I saw him walking out of the lunchroom with his tray of lunchroom food. He had on a yellow and white checkered button-up shirt, slightly baggy khaki pants and brown boots. He walked around the corner and my eyes locked with his and I thought I was just going to melt into the floor. I think my heart skipped a beat and he literally took my breathe away. It was magical.

The second time was when we were driving in my car and I was playfully hitting the senior tassel that every high school graduate gets to hang from their car rear-view mirror (That is, before college starts and you're embarrassed for everyone to know you're a freshman.) In the midst of our playfulness, "somehow" Robert's hand lightly brushed across mine and again, those "butterflies" were so intense that I almost felt sick to my stomach. I'm sure most of you have a very similar story.

Although these are beautiful and fun moments shared between the two of us, the biggest thing to recognize with lust is that it could happen with pretty much anyone. Just like I had those moments of "love at first sight" with Robert; admittedly, I had those same butterflies and feelings with every crush I had during my teen years. Then after a few weeks, I would grow slightly disgusted by my object of affection and move on. The only difference with Robert was that I never grew slightly disgusted with him. The intensity of those biological responses subsided after the typical duration of the infatuation-stage (thought to be no more than 18 months to 3 years),[4] but they stuck around long enough for me to actually develop a love for him. So, in essence, I married Robert because he was the only guy that I didn't eventually get disgusted by. Lol. Romantic story of the year.

Follow Your Heart

It's in those intensely-emotional moments that people tend to go blind and throw all logical reasoning out the door. Lust is an emotionally-based experience with no weight to consequences, reality or morality.

We're not saying that lust doesn't produce real, genuine emotions. We understand that the emotions derived from lust are intense and can feel more "real" than our everyday realities. However, the fact that we are feeling consumed with an emotion has very little to do with whether or not those feelings are right or will lead us to the right decision. Our emotions are the most susceptible and vulnerable way that the enemy can take us off-track.

Our culture has placed such dependency on our emotions that for some people it has become somewhat of an addiction. Instead of looking for the next hit or drink, they are looking for the next moment that will get them an emotional high. Even if they truly desire to make Godly decisions for their lives, they can be so trapped by their own emotions that the idea of letting go of those emotional highs seems life-threatening. That may seem extreme, but have you ever heard the phrase "I can't live without you"?

Sometimes that phrase is a beautiful statement of love and sometimes it's a statement embodied by the emotions of lust.

The only thing worse than feeling trapped by your own emotions is not even knowing you are trapped at all. That's the state where we find society – blindly following our hearts, sometimes to our demise.

All you have to do is take a look at our movies, magazines and shows and you'll see that everything celebrates emotion over commitment. The mantra to almost every sappy, romantic story is to "follow your heart" and the more forbidden or taboo a love is, the higher the emotional intensity.

The entire philosophy to "follow our hearts" is misguided and absolutely contradictory to what God shows us in His Word. Jeremiah 17:9 says that "the heart is more deceitful than anything else. And is desperately sick, who can understand it?" (NASB) And yet, every piece of advice we get culturally is to trust our hearts. No wonder we're such a broken people. We have based our entire existence on something that is deceitfully fleeting.

I (Gloria) remember sitting in a theater watching the movie "Spanglish".[5] In the movie, there is a husband, a wife and a maid. The husband is a good-hearted guy who is genuinely trying his best to make his marriage work and make sure his children are loved. The wife is a serious psycho-path that no one should ever have to live with. She is cold, shallow, obsessive, selfish and borderline crazy. The maid is a beautiful single mom who is compassionate, understanding, smart and deserving.

The love story that the audience wanted to get was the happy-ending between the husband and the maid. It was a great love story and they would've made a beautiful family filled with love and happiness. However, at the end of the movie, before anything irreparable happened, the maid made the determination that she would not be "that woman" and she packed her bags, took her daughter and left. And the husband went back to his house with the psycho wife – who admittedly showed a sign of hopeful sanity at the close of the film. And that was it. The end.

I hated that ending. Inside, I was screaming "NOOOOO!!!! Why did it end that way, that guy and the maid were perfect for each other and that wife is crazy and she doesn't deserve him!!!" It wasn't the "happy-ending" I wanted.

And then it hit me like a ton of bricks. At that time, Robert and I were intricate parts in establishing a Young Marrieds Sunday School ministry of our little hometown church. I advocated for marriages and the ability for God to restore any marriage – no matter how far removed. When did I get to the point that I allowed society to influence me so much that I would hope for the failure of a marriage in favor of emotional-bliss, even in the context of a movie?

I believe it was in that moment that God planted a seed for "CounterCulture Marriage". It was the first time that God unveiled my eyes and I got a glimpse of how much culture influenced how we lived our lives – even Christians living a Godly lifestyle are not immune to the unguarded influences of the world.

Sex & Romance

We've already discussed how the word "lust" is not just about an intense sexual desire for something - it's an intense desire for anything. That "anything" can be porn, romance novels, getting swept away in a romantic movie, finding yourself daydreaming about a man or woman that's not your spouse – whether you know that person or not.

You can lust for almost anything. And we, especially as a Christian culture, hit the nail on the head regarding the dangers of porn and tend to let the romance novels and obsessions to fantasy-based films slide. But those things are just as lustful and just as wrong.

Some people are more visually-sex driven and some people are more emotionally-romance driven. But the sex drive and emotions both stem from the same thing – flesh. You may not be dwelling on and spending your time indulging in visual pictures of pornographic material, but that doesn't mean that you are any less engaged in lustful and damaging behavior.

Women feeding their emotional urges for romance and drama is absolutely no different than a man fulfilling his sexual desires through porn. No. Different. It's exactly the same sin. You are feeding an unhealthy appetite – chasing one high after another.

And just as sex is a gift for married couples, it is the same with emotions. Our emotions are a gift, but when we start perverting sex and perverting our emotions we turn something that was meant for beauty into a disaster.

Is it Lust?

If you are wondering whether you are making choices based on lust, there's an easy measuring stick that you should utilize in every decision.

> *"For out of the heart comes evil thoughts – murder, adultery,*
> *sexual immorality, theft, false testimony, slander"*
> *-Matthew 15:19 NIV*

This verse classifies many things as "evil": murder, adultery, sexual immorality, theft, false testimony and slander. So if the decision you make will eventually lead you to one of those "evil" items, then you are dealing with lust. You can safely disregard what you are feeling and make your determination based on scripture alone.

No One is Immune

Years ago, we spoke with a couple that were dealing with an affair that the husband was having. The wife spoke to one of the husband's female friends that supported his affair and the response the wife was given was, "God wants him to be happy and he's happy with that other woman, don't you want him to be happy too?"

The statement sounds absurd typed out on this page. However, it is exactly how most people in our culture live their lives. What's even more sad is that the temporary happiness that husband would have gotten from being with that other woman doesn't even scratch the surface of the joy and peace he would receive doing it God's way. The advice given wasn't Biblical or accurate. It was just justification for temporal fulfillment.

When you are operating out of lust, you'll use everything to justify what you're doing. The standard justification is spouse-blaming: that someone has "fallen out of love" with their spouse, their spouse doesn't have sex with them, their spouse isn't romantic or doesn't open up emotionally, etc. Everyone is looking for justification for their sins and because no one is perfect, most people can conjure up justification that seems legitimate.

We've read countless articles stating that the cause of affairs or porn addictions begins with something lacking in a marriage. But that would be equivalent to saying that Christians find themselves sinning because God is not perfect – which we all know is not the truth. Granted, our spouses are not perfect by any means, but if humankind is capable of betraying and hurting God even when He provides all that we need, then it is a foolish notion to think that a person's affair, porn addiction or romance obsession develops exclusively because their spouse wasn't satisfying them in some way or because their marriage is lacking.

We're not saying that there aren't things that a spouse could've changed to have made it easier for a person to stay faithful in their thoughts and behaviors, but these issues can develop in marriages where the "innocent" spouse is blameless as well as in marriages where there is something lacking. Lustful behaviors have everything to do with the person committing the sin and very little to do with their spouse's ability or inability to adequately satisfy them.

Even the strongest, most fulfilled marriages are susceptible to the temptations of our flesh. The moment that we start believing that we are above a temptation, is when we let our guards down and the enemy can strike most effectively to catch us off guard.

Realizing how easily the enemy can find his way into our lives and how easily we can fall into temptation, especially given the convenience of the right person/product in the right circumstances for long enough, we can begin to understand why living life in active communion with God, with our guards up and guidelines and accountability in place is so crucial to the success of overcoming or avoiding temptation. Sometimes, circumstances that make sinning convenient are the enemy and sometimes, we put ourselves in those circumstances. We have to constantly be aware of not only "not sinning", but what circumstances we allow to exist in our lives that could be a breeding ground for sin.

The enemy is actively pursuing us with some area of the lust of the flesh. If we take a passive-aggressive approach to defending our lives, the enemy will win. If the enemy actively pursues us, we must actively be pursuing God and keep our watch for the doors that we allow to be opened in our thoughts and behaviors. Always weakening our flesh and strengthening our spirits.

Something New

If you've maintained a great, close marriage with eyes and heart only for your spouse, then more than likely, you feel fulfilled in this area of your life. However, if you are like the majority of marriages around the world and have allowed porn or extra-marital lusts into your marriage, then you've allowed a new emotional or sexual experience to enter into your marriage. Unfortunately, that's one thing your spouse can never be for you – something new and undiscovered. Once they have been "new" they can never be "new" again.

That feeling of discovering something new was intended to be an emotion that God uses to ignite a budding relationship between you and your spouse. When you step out of your marriage and decide to reignite that "new" feeling with someone or something else instead of nurturing it within your marriage, you invite the conflict of comparison into your life and your spouse is setup against impossible odds. The desire for something new will always lead you to go to the next level to continue to experience something new – it's a never fulfilling experience that will eventually leave you broken.

It goes all the way back to the Garden of Eden. Adam and Eve had everything they could ever hope for and were completely fulfilled. But the temptation of discovering something new and having their eyes opened to a world of the knowledge of good and evil was a temptation that they didn't overcome. Yes, their eyes were opened and they certainly discovered many things that were new, but with that discovery also came the introduction of evil in their lives which led to a world of suffering and pain for everyone that followed.

Was it worth it? I think if we were to go back and ask Adam and Eve if discovering something new was worth losing the perfection of the Garden of Eden, their answer would be a resounding "no". We don't always understand what we risk by being disobedient or opening doors of curiosity until it's too late. It's important to trust that God knows what He's doing and His desire is to protect us from experiencing the pain, struggles and regrets that sin can bring with it. It's not worth it.

As illustrated with our dog metaphor earlier in this chapter, if you submit yourself in obedience to God's Word, your emotions will follow suit. Not overnight, but over time, lust will fade away and operating in love will become who you are and you'll never want to go back. Something real will bring so much more depth and fulfillment than the temporary exhilaration of something new.

Passionless Marriage

We can all agree that at some season in your marriage, when your marriage is no longer new, the butterflies will fade. They may come and go, but they don't stay as intense as the infatuation stage of your marriage. So what do you do then? Nobody wants to live in a passionless marriage but you've also made a commitment to be with your spouse forever.

We've found that there are four courses of action that a person takes when they feel the passion has disappeared from their marriage: 1. they find that passion with someone else 2. they blame their spouse, directly or indirectly and continue to live in this state of blame 3. they ignore it and simply get along as amiable roommates or contentious roommates or 4. they pursue a deeper spiritual love.

There may be other methods of coping with the transition from infatuation to love, but they all pretty much fall into one of these four categories. The choices look pretty devastating, except for one.

LOVE
In the context of marital relationships, where lust leaves us unsatisfied and constantly wanting for more, love leaves us feeling satisfied and fulfilled. Love is the third type of connection we discussed earlier – a spiritual connection.

Defining Love
In Hebrew, there are three words associated with "love": "eros", "phileo" and "agape". These three words directly correlate with the three parts of our being (body, soul, spirit) and the three ways that we relate to people (sexually, mentally and spiritually).

"Eros" is about an intoxicating type of "love" and could sometimes be translated as our English word "lust" but without the insinuated perversion of the word "lust". It's the overwhelming feeling we get when we "fall in love" with someone.

"Phileo" is another way of saying "I'm attracted to you and I feel something for you". It's a friendship-based "love" that insinuates that there is a connection with someone. It's what would be used when we say we are "kindred-spirits" with someone or "soulmates" (in romantic relationships and friendships).

Finally, there's "agape" love. This is divine love at a spiritual-level. When the Bible says "God is Love", it's saying that God is "agape". It's not an emotion or a feeling, it's the self-sacrificing nature of giving oneself for someone else.

Since we only have one word in English for "love", in most Biblical translations, these three very distinct words are most often translated into our one English word "love". It's an accurate translation but can cause some confusion when we are trying to figure out whether or not we "love" our spouse or how to continue to "love" our spouse.

For clarity's sake as we use the word "love" in this chapter, we'll define "love" as a self-sacrificing commitment to someone that trumps any conflicting emotions.

Love is not an Emotion

Love can exist completely void of emotion. For instance, we often use the word "care" as a less intimidating way to express the Biblically-defined word "love". Generally, if we care about someone, we are concerned about their well-being, even when it has no bearing on our existence.

In Matthew 22:39, we are commanded to "'love your neighbor as yourself.'" That doesn't mean that we need to have an emotional connection with our neighbor, it means that we are commanded to genuinely and self-sacrificially care about them. Whether it's your grumpy grandfather that you don't like, but still love or the starving children in a third-world country – you can care about someone without experiencing an influx of emotions towards them.

What's the difference between the love/care that we have for other people and the love we have for our spouse and how do our emotions play into it all? The difference lies primarily in how mentally connected we are with someone. We "feel" like we love our spouse and our family more than the starving children in Africa because we have a greater mental connection with them. Remember that our mental connection is our "soul connection" which includes our mind, will and emotions. So the more connected we are with someone mentally, the more our emotions get involved and the greater capacity of our love towards them.

Love is never-ending and has no limitations. However, our soul has a limited supply – we can only create a limited amount of soul connections with people. This is largely part of why, when you foster a mental connection with someone who is not your spouse, your mental connection with your spouse diminishes – further exacerbating the idea that you are "falling out of love" with your spouse.

In the same vein, if our soul is our mind, will and emotions and having a mental connection produces emotions that direct our will, then fostering a greater mental connection with someone is a key to fostering a deeper loving relationship.

Love is not an emotion. Love is a selfless command. Within marriage, it is a self-sacrificing commitment to someone that trumps any conflicting emotions.

Is it Love?

If you're having a hard time determining whether you are operating in love or not, apply the same strategy as when you determined if you were operating in lust or not.

> "Love is patient, love is kind. It does not envy, it does not boast, it is not proud. It does not dishonor others, it is not self-seeking, it is not easily angered, it keeps no record of wrongs. Love does not delight in evil but rejoices with the truth. It always protects, always trusts, always hopes, always perseveres."
> -1 Corinthians 13:4-7 (NIV)

That's a long list. I beg you to not just skim over that passage but read it again and carefully determine what love is. If a behavior that you are considering does not reflect one of the elements in I Corinthians 13, then you aren't acting out of love.

How do we explain the people who have an affair and decide to leave their spouse and marry the "other person" and end up having a genuinely loving second marriage? How do we explain people who say they "married the wrong person" and live a satisfying life, filled with real love, after divorce?

It is our personal belief that there is not only one person on the planet that can become your "soulmate". As we've explained in this chapter, "soulmates" are created by deep mental connections and those connections can probably be fostered with several different individuals if given the opportunity.

That doesn't mean that God doesn't have a mate that He has chosen for you in His perfect will, it just means that the person you marry may not be the only person in the universe that you are capable of having a "connection" with. Simply finding someone else that seems to meet the criteria of "soulmate" doesn't mean that you married the wrong person. It just means, you circumstantially ran into someone else that has the attributes of someone who you would have been compatible with had it been God's will. When we make it more complicated than it is, that's when we start to make foolish decisions because we believe there is some quintessential reason for anyone who enters our life. God can use every encounter with an individual to grow you, but not everyone you encounter is there by divine appointment. Some people just enter your life because they happened to get coffee at the same coffee shop where you get coffee.

Operating in Love

There is a life-altering difference between "love" and "operating in love". You can "love" something or someone and not be "operating in love". "Love" is an entity that can be applied to anyone of anything in various amounts and depths. You can genuinely "love" someone and still behave in a way that hurts them. "Operating in love" means making decisions that line-up with the scriptural attributes of "love".

For example, it is completely possible to love your spouse and yet, not express any patience towards their shortcomings. Just because you did not show your spouse patience when you should have, does not necessarily mean that you do not love your spouse – it means that in that moment, you were not operating in love towards your spouse. See the difference?

A person can love their spouse and at the same time feel love for another person because they have allowed a shift in their mental connection to transfer away from their spouse. They are not operating in love as scripturally commanded and should realign their spirit in accordance to God's Word and their soul will eventually follow suit.

Understanding the difference between "love" and "operating in love" can truly make all the difference.

BUILDING A MARRIAGE ON LOVE

A marriage founded on lust is a marriage built on ever-changing emotions, but a marriage built on love is built on God and that foundation will always remain constant. We've spent the last ten chapters diving into what a marriage built on God looks like through God's Word foundationally and circumstantially, but those things are difficult to keep in check if we are led by what we feel and not by what we know to be true.

Protecting your Heart

The best way to prevent yourself from having to battle with the wrong emotions is to prevent yourself from developing those emotions to begin with. Like Benjamin Franklin once said, "an ounce of prevention is worth a pound of cure."

It's definitely not a popular concept these days that married people shouldn't have friends of the opposite sex. Most people in the world would consider that to be an ultra-conservative rule. We'll admit, we see nothing that would indicate that having friends of the opposite sex is a sin in any way. The problem is not with the friend, it's with what you are nurturing.

It might start out harmless and casual, but if you begin making it a habit to confide in someone else, to develop memories with someone else, to develop an entire persona and set of friends apart from your spouse, then eventually the transition to developing emotions towards someone else isn't such a far jump.

My (Gloria) sister told me a funny story awhile back. She was answering the phones at our church one day and received a call from a woman wanting to speak to a female pastor. Our church always has a pastor assigned the responsibility of caring for people needing help or prayer on any given day. The assigned pastor that day, however, was a male. When offered the option to speak with the pastor on-call the woman stated that she could not speak to a man because she was married.

My sister, being the very inquisitive soul that she is, prodded for clarification. It turned out, the woman wasn't just requesting to speak with a female pastor, she literally would not SPEAK to a man. She believed that married women should never directly communicate with a male.

Now, we're not suggesting anything that extreme. Honestly, I don't even know how you would make it through a normal day with this type of rule. However, we are saying that there should be some boundaries for your relationships with people of the opposite-sex.

There are always exceptions to the rule, but for the vast majority of scenarios, we've found that one of three things happen when you continue to foster a relationship with a comparable person of the opposite-sex: you develop an attraction or a preference for company with that friend instead of with your spouse, your friend develops an attraction for you (whether they admit it or not) or it causes insecurity, strife or an unseen division in your relationship with your spouse.

Any one of these three things can cause a significant problem in your marriage. Unfortunately, by the time you discover that one of these three things have happened, the situation is a huge ordeal.

It's up to you and your spouse to determine the boundaries for your marriage. Every marriage is different and we don't want to mandate our own personal rules on your marriage if it's not Biblically-mandated. However, in our own marriage, our rules are that those friendships do not exist. We are friendly with people we work with and hang out in groups, but it is never permitted for either one of us to "hang out" with someone of the opposite-sex on our own.

We even go as far as mandating this for business relationships. Because I (Robert) am a pastor, the church I work with mandates the same type of rules and I never expect to have to tell my boss why I can't have a business-lunch with a female co-worker.

However, this wasn't always the case. Before being called into ministry, I worked in sales and there were times that I had to explain to my boss why I could not drive 4-hours out-of-town or be on overnight trips with an attractive female co-worker to wine and dine a client together. My boss didn't understand because he didn't hold the same values, but I didn't get fired and other arrangements were made so that the job could be completed without my having to put myself in a compromising situation. These are the times that we must pray for wisdom and discernment. Not every situation will be the same or can be handled the same way.

In Gloria's line-of-work, business lunches, interviews over coffee and business trips with a colleague or partners are expected. It hasn't been easy to maintain our boundaries, especially since "business lunches" are so justifiable. But those business lunches are all the enemy needs to plant seeds of division in your marriage. Thankfully, we've been able to find discreet workarounds every time that scenario comes up – skype interviews, driving separately, including an extra person at the lunches, etc. Colleagues do not always know the reason for the alternative arrangement, but they've never questioned it.

Gloria's been in the entertainment business for over ten years and there has only been one scenario that we couldn't find a suitable workaround for.

That's one in over ten years. So as justifiable as it may seem, we know that in most cases, developing a personal relationship with a co-worker of the opposite sex is highly avoidable if you genuinely want to.

Having a friend, especially a close friend of the opposite-sex is not a sin, but not necessarily wise. If you set your boundaries right on the border, then when you have a momentary lapse of judgement, you've already failed. But if you set boundaries as far from the edge as possible, then you set yourself up with warning signs and red flags that can ultimately save your marriage from having to work through devastating failures. We know it's those early warning signs that saved our marriage on several occasions.

Protecting your emotions is not just about affair-proofing your marriage. We need to protect our emotions from getting attached to anything that draws us away from God and our spouse and those objects of affection are not always people.

Target your Emotions

As we've stated earlier, God's love is never-ending. God's love through you is never-ending. But your emotions have limitations. You can't pour all your emotions into your spouse and also pour all those emotions into someone or something else.

Earlier in this book, we explained how to prove your priorities practically earlier in this book using the illustration of a "priority bucket". The same illustration can be used here but instead of a priority bucket, we have jars of emotions and let's say that those emotions are represented by little pebbles.

Everyone and everything has a jar full of emotional pebbles they can give away and everyone and everything has an empty jar that can be filled with someone else's pebbles. You can move your pebbles around however you please, but the pebbles you have are limited. You cannot make more pebbles.

When you are married, we assume that you poured all your pebbles into your spouse's jar and your spouse poured all their pebbles into your jar.

But after a while, you make the decision to take one of your pebbles out of your spouse's jar and put it into someone else's jar or into porn's jar. Then let's say that that something else who has been getting your emotional pebbles, starts filling up your jar with their pebbles, filling it up so that there is no more room for your spouse's pebbles.

What's happening here? When you give your emotions to someone or something else, you no longer "feel" those emotions for your spouse. When someone or something else is filling your jar with their pebbles, you no longer have room enough to recognize or receive your spouse's pebbles. Even if they are perfect and are pouring their love out on you, you can't receive it because you have allowed someone else to fill your jar with their emotions for you.

So really, when you make the statement that you are no longer "in love" with your spouse, typically, you've done it to yourself. Somehow, something else got your emotions (pebbles) – kids, busy schedule, the need to take care of everything and everyone, porn, career, etc.

It's not always bad things that you've poured your emotions into. You are supposed to pour your emotions into your children, but if you pour all your emotional pebbles into your child's jar then you don't have anything left for your spouse.

It's all about balancing and distributing your emotions appropriately. If you are unhappy about how you feel towards your spouse, stop and think about where you put all your pebbles and take them back. We have to be intentional about where we are pouring our emotions and who's emotions we are receiving.

GETTING YOURSELF OUT OF A PIT

So what do we do if we are already trapped in our lusts? How do we get out of it? We'll briefly go over some key points here, but if this is something that you are struggling with, we strongly encourage you to get counseling or look into other books that focus exclusively on these topics. Two of our favorites are "Every Man's Battle" by Stephen Arterburn and "Every Woman's Battle" by Shannon Ethridge. For now, here are some key steps to take on your mission to recover your emotional well-being.   Admit It. The first step to recovery is admitting that your emotions are not where they are supposed to be. In other words, confess your sins. Stop justifying your emotions or attraction to someone or something else, stop denying that what you are feeling or struggling with is "normal". Don't blame anyone else. Recognize that you have a problem that needs to be fixed.

Accept It

Once you've admitted that you have a problem, you have to accept it. It's easy to immediately fall into despair because we don't know how to fix our problem. We now realize that we are trapped and we can't simply hide our struggles by going back to that emotional high or image. Understand that changing your emotions doesn't happen instantly, but during the process, know that God still loves you and accepts you. You have to believe that you are forgiven and there is light at the end of the tunnel.

Avoid It

Avoid whatever is fueling your extra-marital lusts or depleting your emotions for your spouse. In spiritual terms, repent – or turn away from it. This means cut-off all aspects of that thing from your life – whether that be physically, emotionally, digitally or in your thinking.

Focus It

Once you rip something out of your life by avoiding it, you'll simultaneously need to fill that void with something else. Stay focused on your relationship with God and His will for your life. The more you focus on your personal relationship with God, His purpose for your life and His guidance, the more that the emotions that used to overwhelm you, will get weaker.

Guard It

Recognize your weaknesses and set limitations appropriate for you. Once it's over, don't let your guard down. Use wisdom. We do not live in the past, but we do need to learn how to make wise decisions for our individual situations. It was Andy Stanley who put it so eloquently when he stated, "In light of my past experience, current circumstances, future hopes and dreams, what's the wise thing for me to do?"

COMMIT YOURSELF

If marriage is just about "being in love" and making us happy, we'd have to get a new marriage every 2-3 years. But God has called us to be committed to our spouses through every season, regardless of how we may feel.

We go through several seasons in our lives and marriage and each season can look a little different. Instead of allowing the circumstances of our lives to draw us apart, we need to continually make sure we are placing our emotions where they need to go and making decisions based on love and not lust. This way, although we change and our circumstances change and even our emotions change, we stay rooted in love and this commitment forces us to evolve more into the "one flesh" that we were created to be.

YOU + ME = ONE

#commitment

culture • A successful marriage is one that manages to not get divorced
counter-culture • A successful marriage is one where
love, joy, peace, unity and purpose are constant

twelve

YOU + ME = ONE

What makes a successful marriage? Is the couple who has only been married five years disqualified from knowing how to have a successful marriage? Does a successful marriage mean that there are no more arguments? Or that the couple lives in a continual state of bliss? Does the couple that's been married 50 years automatically get awarded with a successful marriage award? The answer to each of these questions is, "that depends."

A successful marriage is not defined by the length of time you've managed not to get a divorce or by the level of your happiness. It's not limited to your lack of marital experience or how much or how little you discuss differing opinions with your spouse.

A couple who's been married 50 years may just not have the energy to change their lifestyle even though they are incredibly unhappy – or at least not incredibly happy. The couple who's incredibly happy in their marriage may be happy because each spouse has agreed to allow the other to do whatever they want, no questions asked. The couple who never argues, may truly be on the same page all the time or they may have chosen to stop communicating with each other at all and the couple who's been married 2 years may not have much marital experience but they learned to obey God's Word as it applies to their marriage and therefore have reaped the benefit of a successful marriage early on.

If you want to determine whether or not someone has a successful marriage, we have to look beyond what's on the surface. A truly successful marriage is measured by how quickly you are able to operate in unison with your spouse in obedience to God.

DOES MARRIAGE COME WITH AN OPTION?

Over the last several years we've been made bizarrely aware of how divided our culture encourages us to be within our marriages.

We were reading a well-touted financial advising magazine several years ago and one of the articles emphasized the need for each spouse to have separate financial accounts in the event that something went wrong within the marriage. Memes, articles, blogs and virtually any medium in our culture echo this philosophy with passion. What would happen if their passion was poured into emphasizing the importance of commitment in marriage rather than preparing for its failure?

Somehow over the decades, the institution of marriage has become such a casual thing that it's not much more of a commitment than starting a business, choosing an education major, buying a house with a 30-year mortgage or choosing a career. They are all major decisions that could very well require a lifetime commitment and a lifetime of consequences. The difference between those decisions and marriage is that those decisions, even though life-changing, can be changed and in many cases, should change over your lifetime – which merits the need for back-up plans and other options.

If we Parented like we Married

What if we viewed the decision to become parents the same way we have now come to view marriage? Putting all extreme cases aside, let's assume that you and your spouse have been praying for years for a child of your own and then you finally find out you are pregnant! You both spend nine months being excited and planning for the big day and then the big day arrives and despite the pains associated with childbirth, you and your spouse are on top of the world. Everyone is healthy and everything is perfect. You know there will be tough times ahead, but nothing can compare to the bliss you feel in that moment.

A couple years later, you enter into the potty-training terrible twos and your sweet, loving baby has somehow turned into this crazy little person that demands their way, gives nothing in return, never listens and exhausts you to the point of a constant meltdown day after day after day.

Now you are having second thoughts about your decision to have a child. This wasn't what you expected. You can't go backwards, so you have to figure out another plan. You love your child and are still committed to them, but now there's a possibility that they may never grow out of their terrible two tantrums and you think to yourself that if they don't change in a couple years, you don't think you're going to be able to live. After all, sometimes, you have to make sure that you are a priority and you have to consider your well-being first.

So the next day, you go to the bank and open up an account and start saving. What are you saving for? A rainy day, of course, because that's the next logical thing to do! In the event that your child does not mature out of their tantrums and selfish ways, you've determined that you will need to save up enough money to pay the legal fees and pay for the expenses of searching for the absolute perfect parents to adopt your child. Given the hell that your child has put you through, you know you'll probably have to pay someone else to adopt them instead of the other way around.

As your emergency account grows, so does your child. They are now five and although some things have changed, it has simply taken too long to show any real signs of improvement and you're expecting another child - who will hopefully be much better than your first child. But emotionally, you just can't handle both. So you pack up your child's things, take them by the hand and walk them to the adoption agency. You take out your checkbook and your pen and are so relieved that you thought ahead to save for this moment. You write that check and hand it, along with your child, to the life-saving woman behind the counter. Say goodbye and walk away.

It breaks your heart, but it had to be done. You learned many important lessons and you'll be able to do better the second time around. The most important lesson you've learned is that you should always have a back-up plan.

Marriage is Not a Lesser Commitment

There's not much else to say about that scenario. For the vast majority of us, the scenario above is absolutely absurd. To even think of it on those terms doesn't seem relatable, realistic or logical.

And yet. It's exactly how many people handle their marriages. The argument may be that having children is a much more serious commitment than getting married. But not in God's eyes.

When you are married, you become "one flesh" (Mark 10:8). You no longer "have authority over [your] own body but yields it to [your spouse]" and vice versa (I Corinthians 7:4). You are so intertwined into each other's beings that it is commanded that "no one separate" you (Mark 10:9).

Children on the other hand are only with you for a short time. When they find a spouse they "will leave [their parents] and be united to [their spouse]" (Ephesians 5:31). When children grow older, it is Biblical for them to "make some return to their parents…" (1 Timothy 5:4) which implies that they no longer live alongside their parents but live their own separate lives and only "return the favor" so-to-speak as adults. Children are "arrows in the hands of a warrior" (Psalm 127:4) for you to raise and then send off to fulfill their own God-given destinies.

Children may come through our flesh biologically and we may be willing to give our lives for them, but we aren't called to operate as one being with our children our entire lives. We are called to walk in unison with God and with our spouse – our children on the other hand, will develop their own identities in unison with God and with their own spouses. Children are who we are commissioned to raise for a season, our spouse is part of who we are in Christ.

Our spouse should not take the place of us finding our identity and fulfillment in Christ as individuals, but God has called us to so completely unite that our existence with our spouse is so intertwined with each other that it is not possible for us to separate ourselves from our spouse.

LIVING AS ONE

Remember that when you married, you and your spouse became one. This becoming of one flesh didn't just mean that you shared the same last name, changed your marital status and file your taxes differently. It also didn't just mean that you physically engaged in sex which simulates the becoming of one. Going a step further, it also doesn't only mean that your lives would forever go in the same direction or that you somehow include your spouse in absolutely everything you do. All of these things are true in a sense but becoming one flesh goes a step further. It means that we are no longer to live separate lives while trying to include each other. We are now commanded to live one life, together!

It means you are no longer your own person apart from your spouse. Much like when you get saved, your spiritual identity is in Christ as Christ is in you, when you get married, your identity will forever be connected to who your spouse is. Yes, you are still a unique individual, but after marriage, who you are as an individual should not take precedence over who you are in connection to your spouse. Your individuality is used to complement your spouse's individuality so that the outcome is one marriage, "one being" in perfect unity.

ONE FLESH

To emphasize this, the Bible makes it clear that when you get married, the statement, "it's my body" is no longer valid. Even though physically, it's your biological mind that controls how you lift your leg to walk or which direction your head turns, metaphysically, you relinquish your authority to make those decisions apart from your spouse.

> *"The wife does not have authority over her own body, but the husband*
> *does; and likewise also the husband does not have authority*
> *over his own body, but the wife does."*
> *–I Corinthians 7:4 (NASB)*

Some people may find it beneficial to put a big bold period after that first statement, "the wife does not have authority over her own body, but the husband does." But it's not a period, it's a semi-colon because marriage is not about one person getting to control what their spouse does at all times as in a master-slave scenario. It's about both spouses having the authority to dictate what the other spouse does according to their individual roles within the marriage.

> *"For this reason a man shall leave his father and mother, and the two shall*
> *become one flesh; so they are no longer two, but one flesh."*
> *–Mark 10:7-8 (NASB)*

"One" is defined as "singular" and "flesh" is defined as a "living organism." So we can say that when we marry, we become "one living organism." Obviously, you are still physically two "skin and bone" bodies, but metaphysically, can you say that you and your spouse operate as if you are one living organism? Two physical bodies capable of handling different tasks and being in different locations but operating with the same spiritual brain?

Just as your body no longer belongs to you, the same is true for other "parts" of you. Your thoughts, actions, material possessions, emotional hurts, your past baggage – these no longer belong to just you either. They now belong to your spouse. If you have a problem, then your spouse now owns that same problem and it's now up to both of you to find a solution.

What does it look like practically?
Ok. So we're two different people with two different bodies and two

different personalities, but somehow, we are supposed to be "one flesh" and live our lives as one being?

Does that mean we tie our legs together as if we're starting a three-legged race and never physically separate? Although that would be funny, that's not the case. The way you practically embody becoming "one flesh" with your spouse is difficult to explain and may look different for each marriage.

It's a mindset in how you approach everything you do. You both have your own separate tasks, but you are not separate. It's a transition from having a lifetime of operating as your own self, to now having to function in the same step as someone else. If you are having a hard time grasping what this looks like, here's some practical examples to help you get started:

Appreciate your Differences

Your spouse's differences are what balances you out so that your "one flesh" can be a whole being. We're sure we don't have to tell you that you are different than your spouse. But instead of getting aggravated that your spouse is so different, work together so the gap between your differences diminishes and pushes you both to a perfect unity.

For instance, if you are painfully shy and your spouse is outrageously outgoing, then learning to operate in unity brings you into perfect balance, but you have to be operating together for this to work.

Let's say you and your spouse attend a social function and you immediately go grab some punch and a handful of crackers and cheese dip, find yourself a cozy seat in the corner behind the open propped door and settle in to people-watch through the door window, secretly hoping no one will see you and feel like they have to come talk to you. Your spouse on the other hand, flamboyantly bounces into the room and starts laughing and telling jokes from one group of people to the next – each group lighting up when your spouse joins them but relieved to get back to their conversations when your spouse jumps to entertain the next circle of best friends – never stopping to have any real conversations or listen to someone else's stories.

At the end of the night, your spouse comes and finds you and you both head out the door.

You are a married couple that spent the entire evening enjoying yourselves out together. But not really. Because you didn't spend any time together and you didn't really benefit from the whole "one flesh" concept. You're still just as awkwardly shy and your spouse is just as obnoxiously outgoing.

Take the same scenario. Instead of coming in through the doors and going your own separate ways, try operating in unison – balancing out each other's differences – complementing each other to form a perfect being.

Let's say you both grab some snacks and go from group to group together. Your socially aggressive spouse forces you out of your corner to at least be seen amongst people and listen to what they have to say which you repay by discreetly nudging your spouse in the ribs when you observe that the people in the group are getting annoyed with his non-stop chatter – your spouse takes the hint and lets people talk a little.

Now, you can successfully leave the party claiming you've spent the evening together. Not only that, it was you and your spouse TOGETHER that created better versions of yourself – that made you as a unit more fun to be around socially. You challenged each other, kept each other in check and entered each other's worlds.

Dream Together

Adopt your spouse's dream as your own dream. Align your vision with your spouse's. My (Robert) dreams are Gloria's dreams for me and for us, Gloria's dreams are my dreams for her and for us. We each have different dream tasks in life, but we're both just as passionate about fulfilling each other's dreams as we are our own. Not only that, but each of our dreams, although they appear separate in nature on the surface, are actually just different functions of the same dream that we have for ourselves in our marriage. Or I should say, that God has for us in our marriage.

That's the key. Ultimately, it's the dream or vision that God has given us as a couple. God will not give you a calling that requires you to divorce your spouse. We have to separate what is our own dream and what is a God-given dream – because it's very easy to get those two confused. It takes time seeking after God and living in obedience to Him for Him to reveal the tasks that He has ordained for us to accomplish on this earth. Those tasks will never cause you to live in disobedience to God in your marriage.

If you feel called to missions, but your spouse doesn't, it ends up being a trust issue. Being able to trust God to direct your steps and your spouse's steps in the right direction.

Several years ago, Gloria was working as an actor (prior to her becoming a Producer) with no desire for children. I (Robert) on the other hand, wanted a family and just landed a great job making great money at a Fortune 500 company and didn't necessarily want to move away from our church or family. Gloria was getting regular work, but nothing substantial and we had been discussing for years the possibility of moving across the country where she could more aggressively pursue what she felt God had called her to. The discussion was always based around statements similar to "if this is what God has called me to do, then I need to be diligent and do whatever is in my power to do it."

They were life-changing discussions. If we operated like individuals and only "obeyed" God in one area of our life while sacrificing obedience to Him in our marriage, we may very well be divorced right now. After all, it came down to a discussion of who got to pursue their career and family aspirations and who didn't. We couldn't both have children and not have children and we couldn't both stay where we were while I climbed the corporate ladder and move to the west coast where Gloria dedicated herself more to her career. So who got to "win"?

Thankfully, as aggressive as Gloria tends to be, she was submissive in waiting for me to pray over it and get peace about a decision and she also had the spiritual maturity to understand that God would open up the doors in His timing without her having to make anything happen. The final decision? I simply did not feel that God wanted us to move. That meant that Gloria would seemingly have to "give up" her God-given dreams while I pursued mine.

It came down to trust. Ultimately, even though it wasn't the decision she wanted, she trusted that I was trusting in God to lead us or if nothing else, that even if I was making the wrong decision, God would bless her obedience.

Fast-forward almost ten years later and because of some new tax incentives, the entertainment industry has moved aggressively from the west coast to the southeast. Gloria got clarity on her role in the entertainment industry and almost immediately had projects fall onto her lap. I received a call into ministry and a call to further my education – both with and through geographically local entities. In hindsight, no plan that we could have strategized could have even scratched the surface of how God orchestrated things to happen.

It came from dreaming together and trusting God with our decisions and with His timing. We walk in obedience to His Word as well as boldly operating in our biblical roles within the marriage. That's why they call it "faith", because on the surface, most of what God tells us in His Word or in His Spirit look like the end of everything we want in life, but we have to have faith that He is faithful in our obedience. The only way we can miss what God intends for us, is if we stop following His direction.

Synchronize Your Steps

Make no decision without the knowledge and agreement of your spouse. No decision is "your" decision to make. Every decision is made together. Ok, let me clarify. What you eat for breakfast can be your decision – unless of course, you are like me (Gloria) and you've made a terrible agreement with your husband that you can eat ramen noodles only once a week and not for breakfast – in that case, even what you eat for breakfast is not your decision to make.

I (Gloria) was kind of surprised by how individualistic people operate in their marriages. Several years ago, prior to the onset of Instagram, Robert and I had a disagreement about whether or not I should be accepting Facebook requests from people that happen to know him from work but that I didn't really know directly. I'm a minimalist, so I like my Facebook friend's list to be uber-clean – only people that I interact with at least once a year in person is the guideline that I give myself. I give myself the occasional exception, but it's very rare.

On the other hand, Robert felt like it reflected poorly on him if I didn't accept those people because it was rude since he was somewhat of a public figure within our small little community. It's a classic case of productivity vs. people.

It was a light-hearted debate laced with comedic flare, so I took to Facebooking to poll friends. Which by the way, we strongly advise against, so in hindsight, I was wrong in doing so – however, it did make it possible for me to tell this story.

In any case, I was surprised at how serious my Facebook friends took the issue. What I thought would generate like-minded joking, turned into a platform for people declaring their independence from their spouse. Comments like "it's your Facebook page, do what you want" and "He doesn't get to tell you who you can accept as your friends" populated the post.

Which got me thinking. It was a "joke" to me because in my mind Robert absolutely had a say in what I did on my Facebook page - it never really occurred to me how strongly people operated independent of their spouses.

Yes, there are times when you can make decisions independent of your spouse. I do not call Robert to ask how I should do every little thing – what to eat for lunch, what I'm going to work on today, what books to read, how I discipline our children, etc. But even in those small decisions, they are completely in-line with the bigger decisions of how we are handling our lives. In a sense, I am making decisions in alignment with Robert even on the simple things.

I choose to eat avocados and chicken for lunch instead of a $0.99 preservative-filled frozen burrito because Robert and I, together, decided that we need to start eating healthier. I chose to write this book today instead of work on the film I'm currently producing because Robert and I decided, together, that this book was a God-given priority and I needed to force myself to sit down once a week to work towards finishing it. I chose to read Lisa Bevere's book, "Fight Like a Girl" this month (a great book, you ladies should check it out) instead of some novel because Robert and I discussed, together, the importance of always learning and the different things that I'm struggling with during this season (which happens to be finding my place as a female leader versus leading like a man would). I chose to discipline my child's complaining by making him repeat a positive confession instead of giving him a silent time-out because Robert and I, together, have been talking about our son's negative words becoming too big of a habit.

Even the Proverbs 31 wife made decisions herself – what land to buy, where to plant the vineyard, what clothes to make, how much to sell her merchandise at the market for. But given those verses in context with what the rest of the Bible tells us about marriage, we can safely assume that she didn't just up and decide to make those decisions; but behind closed doors, agreements were discussed beforehand with her husband as to what direction those decisions needed to be headed. And it's not just about the wife getting permission from her husband to make those decisions, it goes both ways. The husband needs to be making decisions in-step with what his wife has agreed on.

No decision is your decision alone to make. Every decision is made together as a couple directly or indirectly.

Keeping in Touch

Make contact with your spouse several times a day however you can (call, text, hug, kiss, etc.). We can't possibly live as "one flesh" if we don't connect in some way. There are always extenuating circumstances - like if your spouse is deployed overseas - but we're talking on a day-to-day basis.

If you learn about something interesting or exciting, who is the first person you want to tell? Your best friend, your sister or your spouse? Much of that depends on what the interesting thing is, but if you find yourself constantly calling someone other than your spouse to tell them what happened, you might want to think about why you didn't call to tell your spouse. Going full circle back to the first chapter on friendship – our spouse should be our best friend. They aren't someone we have to put up with, they are someone we should be excited to live life with.

If your argument is that your spouse isn't interested in the same things, then make an effort to be interested in what they are interested. You're in this thing called life together and everything they do, you're a part of and everything you do, they're a part of.

Put Yourself Out There

For the greater good of the whole, make your part more vulnerable by living a life that's totally exposed and held accountable by your spouse.

You cannot lie to yourself or keep secrets from yourself. If you are feeling a certain emotion, you can't ignore that you feel that way (you can, but that's not healthy).

Sometimes part of getting to that "oneness" in marriage is opening yourself up. Becoming comfortable enough with your spouse that there's nothing you are too insecure to share with them.

Most people avoid doing this because it makes them feel vulnerable – open to attack or criticism. However, your marriage should be a safe place and your spouse should be the guard at the gate of that safe place – approaching all your insecurities with encouragement and love instead of anger and judgement. It will be very difficult to experience the security of a marriage in complete unity if you don't first deal with you and your spouse's ability to respond to things in love.

Disagree with Unity

This may sound like a contradiction but living as "one flesh" means being able to even disagree with unity. View your arguments as an opportunity to grow closer together, not draw apart. Disagreeing is a way for you to more fully get to know your spouse and grow closer together.

If you think about your own mind, you'll find this is true with yourself as well. Sometimes you have a certain opinion about something, but you can change your mind or begin to see another perspective to that same situation. Just because you only have one mind, doesn't mean that you don't have internal disagreements with yourself – but ideally, those internal disagreements don't tear you apart. You take the time to think things through to make an absolute determination or you determine that something simply isn't important enough to have to think about or make a determination at all.

For example, having a disagreement with your spouse about what house to buy requires an absolute determination, but whether Macaroni Grill is a better restaurant than Olive Garden might make for good casual conversation, however it's simply not worth the time beyond that. It's ok if you disagree with your spouse on things, but you have to have the mindset that nothing can separate you and your spouse.

If you are determined that you are inseparable, then having the deeper disagreements can serve to strengthen your marriage. Think of your relationship with God. If you simply go to church and do the religious stuff, you are not necessarily benefitting from an intimate relationship with God. But when you finally become broken before God, you are exposing what's in your heart to Him – and hence, providing a platform to draw closer to Him.

We define "brokenness" as communicating with God your disappointments, asking the taboo questions that you can't wrap your head around, confessing what you've done wrong and complete vulnerability, but all these things could be viewed as disagreements with God. When it pertains to our relationship with God, it's difficult to say we "disagree" with God because God is always right. However, we don't always live like that. We make choices contrary to God's Word, essentially disagreeing with Him in our choices which leads us to confession and brokenness before Him – admitting that there is something deeper in your soul that doesn't sit well with you.

It's the same with your spouse. When you enter into a disagreement with your spouse, it is one of the few times in your relationship when you totally expose yourself – your feelings, disappointments, confessions and the hard questions. It's those moments that you go beyond the superficial mask that you wear to get through the day and you really dig deep into your relationship. It's in those moments when you have the opportunity to grow exponentially closer or allow your differences to tear you apart.

Disagreeing with unity starts with making a commitment to unity.

COMMITMENT

It's one thing to talk about how to operate as "one flesh". That part can be challenging but also be fun. It's an entirely different thing when we talk about what commitment is - because commitment, really isn't commitment, until there is a reason to leave. Marriage is not just about being "one flesh", but it's also about staying true to the commitment you made when you gave your vows. Even when your spouse is unbearable, you are still committed.

> *"Therefore what God has joined together, let no one separate."*
> *–Mark 10:9 (NIV)*

If you are committing to not being separated, then you are committing to stay together. Remember that "One flesh" literally means "A singular living organism" and a singular living organism cannot be torn apart without causing near irreparable damage to both parts. If you are on your second or third marriage, we're not saying that God can't bless your current marriage. He can and He will if you walk in obedience to Him starting where you are at now.

Malachi 2:16 says "'the man who hates and divorces his wife,' says the Lord, the God of Israel, 'does violence to the one he should protect,' says the Lord Almighty." Divorce is a violent process and most of the time, the same problems you had in a previous marriage are carried into subsequent relationships.

As we mentioned in chapter six, culturally, we are so quick to check-out of everything. If we don't like what we're watching on TV, we don't wait for the episode to get good, we just change the channel. If we have a big argument with a boss or co-worker, we don't apply any self-control to work amidst the tension, we just get a new job. If we get into a fight with our spouse, we don't want to go through the process of taking time to calm down and discussing it rationally, we want to just leave. Or at least that's what I (Gloria) did.

When Robert and I first got married, I had the tendency to get so mad that I left. I just drove away and then got furious if he didn't come get me. You have to remember that we were still teenagers when we got married, so I think that much of that teenage drama followed us into the first years of marriage.

That all came to an abrupt end when we had our first child. Robert and I had a massive fight. I put on my bedroom slippers, took my keys and stormed out the door. I got into my car, slammed the door and screeched out of the driveway and all the way to the end of the neighborhood. And then the thought hit me, "he has my baby!" I slammed on the brakes, made a dangerous U-turn, slammed the car into park, marched up the stairs and yelled, "I can't even leave because my baby is still in this house!" Robert replied, "well good, maybe you'll stop leaving then." And that was the end of it. I wasn't going to drag the children into the middle of my fight and throw them into the car while they cried out of panic and I most certainly wasn't going to leave "my" baby, so there was no other option for me but to stay – in another room to calm down – but stay nonetheless.

The truth is, it shouldn't have taken a baby for me to not leave when we fought. The concept of being committed should've been in tact before children so much so that leaving was not an option.

When we say our vows we say that we are committed for "better or for worse." When we are at the altar, we can't picture how bad our "worse" could be, but we committed to it nonetheless. What is your "worse"? And are you committed to that "worse"?

God Hates Divorce

God hates divorce. I think that's common knowledge in the Christian arena. Where the confusion seeps in is when we translate that to "God hates the person who gets divorced" and that's not correct. Far from it actually. God doesn't hate you, but He hates divorce because of what it does to His creation.

We love the way the Message translation puts Malachi 2:16:

> *"'I hate divorce,' says the God of Israel. God of the Angel Armies says, 'I hate the violent dismembering of the 'one flesh' of marriage...'"*

God doesn't just hate the act of divorce because He said not to do it and He wants all His children to obey Him. He hates the act of divorce because He knows the pain and suffering that it causes His children and it's not His intention for us to ever have to go through that kind of agony and heartache.

Just about anyone who has been through a divorce will tell you, divorce is a very messy battle and there are emotional and sometimes, logistical, consequences that may never go away. If you are going to choose to spend all your money and resources, effort and tears on something, why not ditch the cultural mentality of leaving and instead, pour all that "divorce" energy into fighting FOR your marriage? Your marriage is worth fighting for!

RESTORATION

We saw a series of photographs a few years ago that were heartbreaking. A photographer had stumbled upon a swallow bird who had gotten hit by a car and was lying dead in the middle of the road[1]. Swallows are known to mate for life and the injured swallow's mate, was literally crying out by its mate's side and would not retreat to safety without it's dead mate. The photographer, not wanting the bird to get injured as the cars passed by, moved the dead bird to the side of the road and continued to photograph pictures. The little bird continued to scream and mourn the loss of his mate for nearly an hour.

It's interesting to us that even a small, seemingly insignificant creature can feel the pain of a mate lost. It's safe to assume that if they can feel the pain of a mate lost, that they could also feel the joy of a marriage in unity.

My guess would be that the benefit a bird has in its relationship with its mate is that their level of comprehension doesn't exceed their level of God-given commitment to their mate. Meaning, they can't think themselves into a divorce. Their relationship with their life-long mate operates the way that God intended it without the intervention of human failure. If only we had the brains of birds, perhaps divorce would be obsolete.

And perhaps it's that simple. God gave us a higher-level of intelligence and free will, it's true. But perhaps the best thing we can do for ourselves is submit our intelligence and our free will to Him so that what God intended for our lives and marriages can be carried out without our erroneous intervention. In that sense, the birds may have it better.

Don't Overcomplicate Things

We tend to overcomplicate things. We base what we believe on what we see around us, but what we don't realize is that what we see is deceiving. The truth is typically found in the realm of the supernatural and only time can prove such a thing.

Most Christians have this type of faith. Faith that God is a good God and He is capable of miracles. We have a lot of Christian going around saying a bunch of great things about God, but I question if they really believe a word of it.

Do you really believe that God is the God of restoration, transformation, new beginnings, second chances, healing, growth, patience, grace and forgiveness? Do you believe He is strong enough to change you, strong enough to change your spouse, loves you and wants the best for you, your children and your marriage? The thing is, if you really believe something, you act on it. If we truly believe that God wants what's best for us and is capable of turning any situation around, then we would follow His directions to get to our desired destination. God has the road map to happily ever after, but if we don't follow His directions, we'll never get there.

FOUR KEYS TO RESTORATION

If you are going through a near-divorce experience with your spouse – or – if you have already experienced the death of your marriage, God can still bring restoration. CounterCulture Marriage is a book focused on the foundations of a Biblical-marriage, but there are countless amazing books dedicated to restoration of marriages. However, if this is the only book you will ever read in regards to your marriage, we'd like to leave you with four key point to think on in regard to God's ability to restore your marriage.

Each Season Passes

The season you are in right now is not permanent. It may be a long season, but it's not a permanent season. Whether it's a great season in your marriage or a near-divorce season, our peace and joy must be founded in God and not our circumstances. In any case, there is hope in understanding that if you stay obedient to God, He will bring you through the storm. T.F. Tenny, an absolutely amazing and highly anointed minister once said it like this, "three men were sent into the fire, but the king saw four in the furnace. Guess what, only three came out. You know what that means? The fourth man was already there when they arrived and He'll still be there the next time they (or you) show up. God will meet you in the fire and He will get you through it!".

Be Obedient

This doesn't just mean to seek His hand (what God can do for us or what He can fix), but it means to seek His face through prayer. Read the Bible and ask God for revelation. Pray consistently throughout the day about your situations. Thank Him constantly for the good things in your life and most importantly, be obedient to what you know He is calling you to do. Don't be stubborn and refuse to let go of something that God is calling you to move past.

Be All-In

As a tie-in to being obedient to God – be "all-in" in your marriage. Do everything you know to do to apply yourself to your marriage Biblically. God can restore your marriage to a place beyond what you've had before, but He can't do that if you refuse to be a part of it. Our relationship with God is about forgiveness, grace and reconciliation – not abandonment. Our entire spiritual existence is founded on those three things – forgiveness, grace and reconciliation. Nothing good can happen apart from those three things.

Nothing is Wasted

He can use your failures to strengthen your marriage. Nothing is beyond repair. Nothing is unusable. Nothing is "so bad" that God can't bring you AND YOUR SPOUSE through it together. In fact, God will use your experience as a testimony to help other people. It's only God who can take the mess you are in now and use it as a platform for the purpose He has called you to.

God can restore any marriage to 100% no matter the trials. But you have to be willing to go all-in, trust Him and do whatever it takes. No pride, no disobedience. If you put obedience to God above your own personal happiness, restoration will come and so will that happiness you wanted in the first place. As Jentezen Franklin puts it, "when you make up your mind that you're not going to quit, that's when the battle is really won".[2]

A GREATER PURPOSE

It's not enough to simply not be divorced. That's not it. The "it" is being able to experience all the glory that marriage was meant to be and that requires us to constantly move closer to our spouse. More importantly, it requires a constant growing closer to God. The more you grow in your relationship with God, the more He molds your character and the better spouse you become.

Don't settle for the "just [staying] married" bumper sticker on your car. Go for the "happily ever after" bumper sticker.

Our marriage and our life are for a much greater purpose than just dealing with our own personal issues. God put us together with our spouse to fulfill a greater calling to influence the world. God uses our marriages to direct His perfect will in our lives.

Giving up your marriage means delaying His ultimate purpose for you. Not necessarily because you did something "bad", but because you may be spending the next several years healing from a broken marriage and it will take that much longer for you to get to the point of being able to focus exclusively on the "what's next" in God's plan. When we're so wrapped up in our own drama, it's difficult for us to see beyond ourselves.

God uses your marriage to transform you as an individual. Having the "happily ever after" in your marriage isn't just about you. It's about using your marriage to influence the world. You are a representative of Christ – as long as a couple stays married they continue to display, however imperfectly, the ongoing commitment between Christ and His church.

Not only that, but your marriage is directly tied to your God-given destiny. God put you together so that you, with your spouse, could become one perfect entity mobilized for His purpose. There is absolutely no greater "happily ever after" than to walk in unity with your spouse toward the destiny God has for you being used by Him to showcase His love for the lost and broken.

Our marriage is metaphorical in many ways. Physically, the coming together as "one flesh" produces fruit. The same thing is true spiritually. If we can find a way to come together and operate as "one flesh" spiritually, we'll be able to face any obstacle head-on, hand-in-hand and we'll be able to produce spiritual fruit – life change in our communities and world together.

"Happily Ever After" absolutely does exist and it's absolutely available to anyone willing to walk in obedience to God's Word. "Counter-culture" is not just a catchy phrase. It's a way of intentionally living apart from the world around us and in pursuit of all that God has for us.

NOTES

Chapter 1: The Business of Marriage

1. Eileen K. Graham, Denis Gerstorf, Tomiko Yoneda, Andrea M. Piccinin, Tom Booth, Christopher Beam, Andrew J. Petkus, et al, "A Coordinated Analysis of Big-five Trait Change Across 16 Longitudinal Samples." *PsyArXiv*, December 19, 2017. https://psyarxiv.com/ryjpc/.

2. Ron Milo and Rob Phillips. *CELL BIOLOGY by the numbers.* (Garland Science, 2015), 330. http://book.bionumbers.org/how-quickly-do-different-cells-in-the-body-replace-themselves/.

3. Aimee Groth, "You're The Average Of The Five People you Spend The Most Time With." *Business Insider,* July 24, 2012. http://www.businessinsider.com/jim-rohn-youre-the-average-of-the-five-people-you-spend-the-most-time-with-2012-7.

4. Meg Selig, "How Do Work Breaks Help Your Brain? 5 Surprising Answers." *Psychology Today,* April 18, 2017. https://www.psychologytoday.com/us/blog/changepower/201704/how-do-work-breaks-help-your-brain-5-surprising-answers.

Chapter 2: What Wo/Men Want

1. Emerson Eggerich. *Love & Respect.* (Nashville, Nelson, Thomas, 2004).

Chapter 3: Dictators

1. Mark Rutland, *21 Seconds to Change the World.* (Bloomington: Bethany House, 2016), 22.

2. Robert Morris, "One Marriage Conference," (sermon, Free Chapel, Gainesville, GA, February 2017).

3. Dove Self-Esteem Fund, "Real Girls, Real Pressure: A National Report on the State of Self Esteem." *ISACS,* June 2008. http://www.isacs.org/misc_files/SelfEsteem_Report%20-%20Dove%20Campaign%20for%20Real%20Beauty.pdf.

Chapter 4: Doormats

1. Blue Letter Bible, s.v. "submit," November 2, 2018, http://www.blueletterbible.org.

2. "Medco Health Solutions Inc.: America's State of Mind: New Report Finds Americans Increasingly Turn to Medications to Ease their Mental Woes; Women Lead the Trend." *Market Screener,* November 16, 2011. https://www.marketscreener.com/MEDCO-HEALTH-SOLUTIONS-IN-13526/news/Medco-Health-Solutions-Inc-America-s-State-of-Mind-New-Report-Finds-Americans-Increasingly-Turn-13893442/.

3. Blue Letter Bible, s.v. "help," November 2, 2018, http://www.blueletterbible.org.

4. Ibid, "suitable"

5. Aesop, "The North Wind and the Sun." *Aesop's Fables.* http://read.gov/aesop/143.html.

Chapter 6: Fighting Fairly

1. Chad Craig, *Divine Design for Discipleship* (Xulon Press, 2008)
2. Jentezen Franklin, *Love Like You've Never Been Hurt* (Bloomington: Chosen Books, 2018), 100.

Chapter 7: More Money, My Money, No Money

1. "Financial Checklist for Newlyweds," *Consumercredit.com*, July 23, 2015. https://www.consumercredit.com/about-us/press-releases/2015-press-releases/financial-checklist-for-newlyweds
2. *Be grateful for what you have!* Produced by Igor Kalashnikov. Bright Side, 2016. YouTube. https://www.youtube.com/watch?v=Eyfa1yR8tx0

Chapter 9: Expect Less, Appreciate More

1. Cynthia Sass, "Why You Really Are What You Eat." *Sass Yourself*, Accessed November 2, 2018. https://cynthiasass.com/sass-yourself/sass-yourself-blog/item/116-why-you-really-are-what-you-eat.html

Chapter 10: Intimate Apparel

1. "Leblouh." *Wikipedia*. https://en.wikipedia.org/wiki/Leblouh
2. Sara C Nelson, "Yaeba: Japanese 'Double Tooth' Trend Will Give You A Costly Crooked Smile," *Huffington Post UK*, January 2, 2013. https://www.huffingtonpost.co.uk/2013/02/01/yaeba-japanese-double-tooth-trend-expensive-crooked-smile_n_2596720.html?guccounter=1&guce_referrer_us=aHR0cHM6Ly9lbi53aWtpcGVkaWEub3JnLw&guce_referrer_cs=iR0Swe0BH12SDZxjgajuRQ.
3. Tracey R Rich, "Kosher Sex," *Judaism 101*, Access November 3, 2018. http://www.jewfaq.org/sex.htm.
4. Sinclair Intimacy Institute, "Clitoris," *How Stuff Works*, 2002. https://health.howstuffworks.com/sexual-health/female-reproductive-system/clitoris-dictionary1.htm.
5. Kara Mayer Robinson, "10 Suprising Health Benefits of Sex," *WebMD*, Accessed November 3, 2018. https://www.webmd.com/sex-relationships/guide/sex-and-health#1

   Sophia Breene, "15 Science-Backed Reasons to Have More Sex," *Greatist*, October 23, 2013. https://greatist.com/health/health-benefits-of-sex

   Stuart Brody, "The Relative Health Benefits of Different Sexual Activities," *The Journal of Sexual Medicine 7, Issue 4 Part 1* (2010) 1336-1361. https://www.jsm.jsexmed.org/article/S1743-6095(15)32977-5/fulltext.
6. "Why Don't Jews Believe in Jesus?" *Simple to Remember*, Accessed November 3, 2018. https://www.simpletoremember.com/articles/a/jewsandjesus/
7. Blue Letter Bible, s.v. "Proverbs 5:19," November 2, 2018, http://www.blueletterbible.org.

Chapter 11: What's Love Got to Do With It?

1. Jentezen Franklin, *Fasting* (Lake Mary, FL: Charisma House, 2007)
2. Klinck, Mary. "All Dogs Need a Job: How to Keep Your Dog Happy and Mentally Healthy," in *Decoding Your Dog*. (Mariner Books, 2015).
3. Blue Letter Bible, s.v. "lust," November 2, 2018, http://www.blueletterbible.org.
4. Susan Heitler, "The Deceptive Power of Love's First Moments," *Psychology Today*, July 13, 2012. https://www.psychologytoday.com/us/blog/resolution-not-conflict/201207/the-deceptive-power-loves-first-moments.
5. *Spanglish*. Directed by James L. Brooks. Los Angeles, CA: Sony Pictures, 2004. DVD.

Chapter 12: You + Me = One

1. Wilson Hsu. *Grief - Barn Swallows*, photo.net, https://www.photo.net/photo/2315290.
2. Jentezen Franklin, *Love Like You've Never Been Hurt* (Bloomington: Chosen Books, 2018), 218.

CPSIA information can be obtained
at www.ICGtesting.com
Printed in the USA
BVHW080058170119
538046BV00002B/3/P

9 780692 091272